947.084
REE

In defence of October

A debate on the Russian Revolution

In defence of October

A debate on the Russian Revolution

John Rees
with
Robert Service,
Sam Farber and
Robin Blackburn

BOOKMARKS

London, Chicago and Sydney

**In defence of October: a debate on the Russian Revolution—John Rees
with Robert Service, Sam Farber and Robin Blackburn**
First published in International Socialism 52 and 55
This edition first published 1997
Bookmarks Publications Ltd, c/o 1 Bloomsbury Street, London WC1B 3QE,
England
Bookmarks, PO Box 16085, Chicago, Illinois 60616, USA
Bookmarks, PO Box A338, Sydney South, NSW 2000, Australia
Copyright © Bookmarks Publications Ltd and International Socialism

ISBN 1 898876 28 2

Printed by BPC Wheatons
Coverby Sherborne Design

**Bookmarks Publications Ltd is linked to an international grouping of
socialist organisations:**
- **Australia:** International Socialist Organisation, PO Box A338, Sydney South
- **Britain:** Socialist Workers Party, PO Box 82, London E3
- **Canada:** International Socialists, PO Box 339, Station E, Toronto, Ontario
  M6H 4E3
- **Cyprus:** Ergatiki Demokratia, PO Box 7280, Nicosia
- **Czech Republic:** Socialisticka Solidarita, PO Box 42, Praha 42, 140 02
- **Denmark:** Internationale Socialister, Postboks 642, 2200 København N
- **Greece:** Socialistiko Ergatiko Komma, c/o Workers Solidarity, PO Box 8161,
  Athens 100 10
- **Holland:** Internationale Socialisten, PO Box 92025, 1090AA Amsterdam
- **Ireland:** Socialist Workers Party, PO Box 1648, Dublin 8
- **New Zealand:** Socialist Workers Organisation, PO Box 8851, Auckland
- **Norway:** Internasjonale Socialisterr, Postboks 5370, Majorstua, 0304 Oslo 3
- **Poland:** Solidarność Socjalistyczna, PO Box 12, 01-900 Warszawa 118
- **South Africa:** Socialist Workers Organisation, PO Box 18530, Hillbrow
  2038, Johannesburg
- **Spain:** Socialismo Internacional, Apartado 563, 08080, Barcelona
- **United States:** International Socialist Organization, PO Box 16085, Chicago,
  Illinois 60616
- **Zimbabwe:** International Socialist Organisation, PO Box 6758, Harare

Contents

John Rees is the editor of *International Socialism*, the author of *The ABC of Socialism* and *The Algebra of Revolution* and a leading member of the Socialist Workers Party in Britain.

Robert Service is the author of a biography of Lenin and *The Russian Revolution 1900-1927*.

Sam Farber is the author of *Before Stalinism*.

Robin Blackburn is editor of *New Left Review* and the author of *The Overthrow of Colonial Slavery*.

1

In defence of October

John Rees

W ill those socialists who most fervently wished for the end of Stalinism also be its last victims? The East European revolutions of 1989 were welcomed by most socialists, particularly those who argued that Stalinism was not the rightful heir of the 1917 October revolution but its perverter and destroyer. Nevertheless, the impact of 1989 has not been to strengthen the general socialist tradition. The very opposite has been the case.

The collapse of the Stalinist regimes has given renewed force to an old argument: that the seeds of destruction were sown in the very first days of the Bolshevik revolution. Predictably, right wingers have seized on the 'collapse of socialism' as a stick with which to beat the revolutionary tradition—from former *Times* editor William Rees-Mogg's bizarre invocation of chaos theory to show that Lenin's struggle to gain control of *Iskra* in 1903 led directly to the gulag, to former US National Security Council member Richard Pipes's widely praised and intensely ideological tome *The Russian Revolution*, the message is the same: Lenin led to Stalin.[1]

In Russia itself a similar but even more profound ideological shift is under way. Once both the Stalinist bureaucracy and the Western ruling classes insisted that Stalinism was socialism. The Stalinists needed the mantle of the revolution to justify their barbarity and the Western capitalists needed to show that revolution could only lead to barbarity. Then they united in arguing that the revolution led to disaster. The Stalinist bureaucracy needed the world market and the Western ruling classes wanted a Russia that was open to the world market. In all cases and at all times these two massive social forces united to exclude the voice of the genuine socialist tradition, the voice which rejected both Stalinism and Western capitalism.

So, just as Pipes was celebrating the White Russian interpretation of the revolution in the West, *Moscow News* devoted its middle pages to accounts of the revolution and civil war taken from archives compiled by Josif Gessen of the Cadets, the bourgeois party in 1917, including pieces written by the mother of White general Baron Wrangel and by Tsarist officers.[2] Meanwhile at the Central Committee printing plant in Moscow in 1992 volumes of Marx and Lenin gave way to biographies of Wrangel, his fellow White leader Admiral Kolchak and Solzhenitsyn's *The Gulag Archipelago*.[3] It is hardly surprising then that socialists in Russia are confronted again and again with arguments which first saw the light of day in White publications from the 1920s, like S P Melgounov's *The Red Terror in Russia*.[4]

But what is new in the wake of the East European revolutions is that many on the left have joined this already substantial chorus. Immediately after the East European revolutions *Marxism Today* editor Martin Jacques said, 'It's the end of the road for Stalinism and most of Leninism. The people have rejected authoritarianism.' Nina Temple, the general secretary of the Communist Party, added, 'If you look at Russia since the revolution, things went wrong from the start'.[5] Historian Eric Hobsbawm believes that, 'For about half a century, from 1914 to the aftermath of the Second World War, the world passed through a period of cataclysm, producing all manner of freak results, of which the Russian Revolution is probably the most long-lasting.' Hobsbawm argues that Lenin shouldn't have made the October revolution:

> There were indeed Marxists—the Mensheviks, Plekhanov, other people—even in Russia who took this view. Old Plekhanov, who was the father of Russian Marxism, suggested to Lenin that all you could produce that way was some kind of socialist version of the Chinese empire.[6]

In *Has Socialism Failed?* and other writings Joe Slovo, general secretary of the South African Communist Party, added his criticisms of the October revolution to the general hubbub, using them as a lever to propel the South African CP along the reformist road that its European sister organisations travelled long ago. In *The African Communist* Slovo wrote, 'Quite a few outstanding leaders of the Bolshevik revolution (including Trotsky, Bukharin, Kamenev and Radek) who came to be "oppositionists" to Stalinism, not only played a significant role in erecting part of its theoretical edifice, but also encouraged some of its practices before Stalin was in the saddle and long before the emergence of an economically privileged strata'.[7] Thus Slovo, who spent every hour of his political career defending Stalinism, accused Trotsky of being responsible for...Stalinism! Rarely can a blacker pot have upbraided a cleaner kettle.

With the Stalinists the umbilical cord that links socialists with the struggle of the working class has been severed for so long that it is unlikely that many of them will find their way back towards the classical Marxist tradition. State worship, the craven bending of the knee before the established fact of a strong state which called itself socialist, was always an important part of Stalinism. Little surprise, then, that once those states collapsed so too did the Stalinists' faith in socialism.

More surprising than the reaction of yesterday's Stalinists is that of the anti-Stalinist socialists who have written about the October revolution in a similar vein. Robin Blackburn, the editor of *New Left Review*, has written that 'Marxism cannot escape implication in the fate of the Russian Revolution'. Lenin cannot 'escape the charge' of having laid the ground for Stalin, in part because Lenin was not, mind you, 'a systematic thinker'.[8] And one time Marxist Paul Hirst has written that Lenin's determination to found a better society was a utopian vision which inevitably led to 'the Bolshevik Party's monopoly of power, to the system of secret police control and to the inherently authoritarian practice of democratic centralism'.[9]

In *Before Stalinism* US socialist Sam Farber argues that Lenin's views and actions '*inevitably and necessarily* led to an elitist form of government' and that the 'Bolsheviks firmly adopted policies that moved them a considerable distance towards what later became the Stalinist totalitarian model'.[10] Farber is a member of the US socialist organisation Solidarity and

9

an editor of its magazine *Against the Current* in which a fierce debate over these and related issues has broken out. At least one contribution is virtually indistinguishable from right wing attitudes to the October revolution.[11]

The same sort of argument has surfaced among oppositionists in Eastern Europe. Adam Michnik criticised 'the "totalitarian temptation" of those activists in Polish Solidarity who wanted the movement to...struggle for state power'.[12] And Moscow socialist Boris Kagarlitsky, in an account generally more sympathetic than many in the West, still claims that 'Lenin's party was to a greater degree the party of Peter I than the party of Karl Marx, since it strove first and foremost to ensure that Russia imitated contemporary forms of Western organisation'. He goes on to argue that the Bolsheviks' 'dictatorial methods scared off the Western proletariat from revolution'. The fact that 'the Bolsheviks did not take into account the indivisibility of democratic principles' was one element in making the rise of Stalin the 'more or less logical' result.[13]

There is clearly a case for revolutionaries to answer. Such an answer must move beyond the general accusation that 'Lenin led to Stalin' and examine in detail the arguments of the Bolsheviks' critics. This involves looking at some of the key questions about the Russian Revolution: Was it a 'premature' revolution? Was the October revolution a coup? Were the Bolsheviks a monolithic party? Were the Bolsheviks right to disperse the Constituent Assembly? What about the Red Terror, the Cheka and Kronstadt?

Such questions are of more than historical interest. The October revolution is the touchstone of 20th century politics. To know an individual's attitude to October is to know whether they stand for capitalism, Stalinism or the genuine socialism of the classical Marxist tradition. As Stalinism collapses the question is posed point blank: is 'reformed' capitalism now the only path the working class can take? To those, like Martin Jacques, who can see only the precursor of Stalinism in the October revolution, the answer is an enthusiastic yes. Those who rot on the dole queues of the Western world, those threatened by slump and war, racism and oppression may not be so quick to agree. They may wish to know why today many socialists rush to join in declaring that Lenin led to Stalin with those who are in every other respect their bitterest enemies.

A 'premature' revolution?

It has once again become fashionable to appeal to the Mensheviks and to Kautsky and Plekhanov, to show that the Russian revolution was 'premature', that the economic conditions in backward Russia could not support the attempt to build a socialist society. This is the gist of Hobsbawm and Kagarlitsky's comments cited above. It is also an important part of Robin Blackburn's case:

> In *The Communist Manifesto a*nd in other writings, Marx and Engels famously insisted that a genuine socialism could only be built on the basis already laid by capitalism; in Th*e German Ideology* they observed that socialism would require social overturns in at least several of the most developed countries. From this classic Marxist conviction it followed that it was a complete delusion to attempt to 'build socialism' in one large and backward country.[14]

This argument is, of course, the ABC of Marxism. Its logic is faultless so long as it is confined to the borders of one country. But already in 1906, in *Results and Prospects*, Trotsky had dealt with this objection in detail. He examined the maturity of Western industry and the Western working class in the section on 'The prerequisites for socialism' and then went on to address precisely the question that Robin Blackburn, using Kautsky as his authority, raises. Trotsky's conclusion was:

> *Without the direct state support of the European proletariat the working class of Russia cannot remain in power and convert its temporary domination into a lasting socialistic dictatorship.* Of this there cannot for one moment be any doubt. But on the other hand there cannot be any doubt that a socialist revolution in the West will enable us to directly convert the temporary domination of the working class into a socialist dictatorship.[15]

In the course of 1917 Lenin and the Bolsheviks adopted this perspective wholeheartedly. Even Stalin could summarise the differences between Lenin, on the one hand, and Zinoviev and Kamenev, on the other, over whether to make the October revolution in these terms: 'There are two lines: one sets the course for the victory of the revolution and relies on Europe, the second does not believe in the revolution and counts only on being an

11

opposition'.[16] In the very midst of the revolution Trotsky, now speaking for the Bolshevik government, repeated his prognosis of 1906:

> If the peoples of Europe do not arise and crush imperialism, we shall be crushed—that is beyond doubt. Either the Russian revolution will raise the whirlwind of struggle in the West, or the capitalists of all countries will stifle our struggle.[17]

And Lenin, in an oft repeated argument, said:

> It is not open to the slightest doubt that the final victory of our revolution, if it were to remain alone, if there were no revolutionary movement in other countries, would be hopeless... Our salvation from all these difficulties, I repeat, is an all-European revolution.[18]

These were not, as Robin Blackburn claims, Lenin and Trotsky's 'later justifications of the original Bolshevik seizure of power'.[19] They were the avowed perspective of the Bolsheviks before, during and after the October revolution. It was, concludes E H Carr, 'the European revolution, on which the confident calculations, not merely of a few optimists but of every Bolshevik of any account, had been based'.[20] And the Bolsheviks were not alone in looking to a European revolution. Even Kautsky, in a passage from 1904 which somehow seems to escape the notice of his modern admirers, acknowledged the possibility of a revolution in Germany which:

> must lead to the political domination of the proletariat in Western Europe and create for the Eastern European proletariat the possibility of contracting the stages of their development and, copying the example of the Germans, artificially setting up socialist institutions. Society as a whole cannot skip any stages in its development, but it is possible for the constituent parts of society to hasten their retarded development by imitating the more advanced countries and, thanks to this, even to take their stand in the forefront of development...[21]

Kautsky's post-1917 critique of the Bolsheviks depended on casting off this creaking premonition of the theory of permanent revolution. By then Kautsky was all too keen to avoid looking at European capitalist society 'as a whole' and to condemn a revolution in one of its 'constituent parts'. Yet even after the October revolution, in the midst of his tirade against the Bolsheviks,

Kautsky could not quite shake off the power of the Bolsheviks' analysis:

> The Bolsheviks must not be too much blamed for expecting a European revolution. Other socialists did the same, and we are certainly approaching conditions which will sharply accentuate the class struggle, and which may have many surprises in store. And if the Bolsheviks have till now been in error in expecting a revolution, have not Bebel, Marx and Engels cherished a like delusion? This is not to be denied.[22]

This perspective was never the baseless optimism of which it is accused by its latter day critics. It was founded on a detailed examination of the way in which the world market, and with it imperialism, had welded the capitalist world into a single organism. It was an organism whose parts were simultaneously shaken by economic crises and racked by war, and in which the great labour unrest of the pre-First World War period had assumed similar intensity in a number of major countries. Lenin and the Bolsheviks were alone in developing a theory of imperialism which could explain the nature of modern capitalism and the international scope of the class struggle which it produced. No other socialists, including left Mensheviks like Martov, even attempted such an analysis.

In the post-war years the Bolsheviks' prognosis was proved absolutely correct. *There was a European wide revolutionary upheaval*. The Easter Rising in Ireland predated the October revolution. The fall of the German Kaiser, precipitated by a naval mutiny and a general strike, followed the revolution in November 1918. More revolutionary crises ensued. As Victor Serge recalls:

> Revolution descended on the streets of Vienna and Budapest… From the Scheldt to the Volga the councils of workers' and soldiers' deputies—the soviets—are the real masters of the hour. Germany's legal government is a Council of People's Commissars made up of six socialists.[23]

In March 1919 a soviet government took power in Hungary and in the same year massive labour unrest shook the British state to its foundations. For 'the two red years' Italy was convulsed by massive class struggles, only brought to an end by what Serge describes as 'a preventative counter-revolution' which brought Mussolini to power.

13

Elsewhere Serge remembers:

> The newspapers of the period are astonishing…riots in Paris, riots in Lyon, revolution in Belgium, revolution in Constantinople, victory of the soviets in Bulgaria, rioting in Copenhagen. In fact the whole of Europe is in movement, clandestine or open soviets are appearing everywhere, even in the Allied armies; everything is possible, everything.[25]

At the other end of the political spectrum, Lloyd George wrote:

> The whole of Europe is filled with the spirit of revolution. There is a deep sense not only of discontent but of anger and revolt amongst the workmen against the pre-war conditions. The whole existing order in its political, social and economic aspects is questioned by the masses of the population from one end of Europe to the other.[26]

It was on the basis of these class struggles, unprecedented in scale and intensity, that the Third International was able to rally to its banner mass Communist Parties numbering hundreds of thousands of members in most European countries. By 1920 the Third International could count on the following organisations: the Italian Socialist Party, 300,000 strong; the Czechoslovak CP, with 400,000 members; the 140,000 of the French Socialist Party; the 35,478 comrades of the Bulgarian Socialists; the 17,000 members of the Swedish Socialist Party; a mass German Communist Party, Norwegian Labour Party and Yugoslav Socialist Party.[27]

What was lacking in these revolutionary upheavals was not the objective European-wide crisis. Neither was it the willingness of workers to struggle for power. What was lacking was a leadership of sufficient clarity and an organisation with a core of sufficiently experienced members to successfully lead these movements to power. This was the decisive difference between the German and Russian revolutions. It was a weakness which the Bolsheviks laboured heroically to overcome in the Third International. It was certainly not a struggle that was doomed to failure in advance.

The Bolsheviks correctly predicted a European revolution and they strained might and main to provide that revolution with a leadership which could bring it to a successful conclusion. They were right to try. As Marx once observed, 'world history would indeed be very easy to make, if the struggle were taken up only on condition of infallibly favourable chances.'[28]

What was Kautsky's attitude to the German revolution? Surely here, in the second most advanced industrial country of the day, none of the arguments about the impermissibility of socialism in backward countries need apply. While Kautsky *opposed* socialist revolution in backward Russia, he would, surely, *support* it in advanced Germany? Nothing of the sort. Kautsky opposed a socialist revolution in the name of capitalist democracy every bit as vehemently in Germany as he did in Russia. He declared Rosa Luxemburg to be every bit as dangerous as Lenin. In debate with Luxemburg a leader of Kautsky's party, Hugo Haase, seemingly oblivious of the contradiction, said:

> We cannot slavishly imitate the Bolshevik revolution here, because the objective conditions are completely different. Russia is a peasant country... Only 10 percent of the population are industrial workers. Germany, on the other hand, is a developed, industrialised state which needs food supplies. The majority of its population are proletarians.[29]

Robin Blackburn is, of course, in the same bind. If the Russian revolution was mistaken because it took place in a backward country, then today, in Britain, the same injunction cannot apply. Yet Robin Blackburn objects just as forcibly to a revolutionary strategy in Britain today as he does to the Bolsheviks' strategy in 1917. The unavoidable conclusion is that all the talk about 'premature' revolution, in Robin Blackburn and Kautsky's cases, is an *excuse* born of expediency, not a serious argument against revolutionary socialism.

October: coup or revolution?

The contrast between the spontaneous mass uprising of February 1917 and the 'Bolshevik coup' of October 1917 is one of the staples of right wing interpretation of the revolution. It is a view which is gaining renewed force from events in Eastern Europe. As one historian has recently observed:

> [The] portrayal of the Bolshevik victory as the product of the organisational skill of a ruthless, conspiratorial minority has

15

informed conventional wisdom in the West for so long that it has made an all but indelible impression on popular assumptions about the revolution. Although recent specialist work has cast doubt upon many of its propositions, studies adhering to it continue to appear and it still provides the common currency of Western media commentary. Moreover, the spectacle of perestroika, of Communism repentant, promises to lend it a new lease of life. The graver the travails of the Soviet Union, the bolder the adherents of [this] view seem likely to become.[30]

Thus for Pipes the revolution was 'a model of a modern coup d'etat'.[31] Few socialists, anarchists apart, have been willing to swallow much of the right wing story. But while they accept that October was a genuine mass rising, they tend to understate the degree to which the Bolsheviks had to fight against *all* other socialist parties to make the revolution possible in the first place. They also tend to underestimate the intense polarisation that the revolution involved, playing down the threat of counterrevolution. Both these arguments are then used to buttress criticisms of the Bolsheviks' post-October actions: their dispersal of the Constituent Assembly and their conduct of the civil war.

But what had brought the Bolsheviks to power? Clearly their programme and tactical flexibility were essential. But that is only part of the story. The remainder is explained by how the other parties responded to the growing crisis. The path from February to October is not the royal road of the Bolsheviks' rise to power, it is also the story of the other parties' steep descent in the estimation of the mass of workers and peasants as they failed to give adequate answers to the most pressing questions posed by the revolution.

The February revolution raised three key issues: the war, the land and the factories. And there were three key political forces: firstly, the old order whose most powerful remnants were the officer corps of the Tsarist army supported, sometimes with reservations, by the bourgeois Constitutional Democrats (Cadets). Secondly, there were the parties of the working class—the Bolsheviks and Mensheviks. Finally there were the Socialist Revolutionaries (SRs), oriented on and thinking of themselves as the representatives of the peasants, though often led by intellectuals, lawyers and other sections of the urban middle classes.

The regime which issued from the February revolution, headed by the Provisional Government, was dominated by the Cadets. It refused to distribute the land to the peasants, vowed to continue the war and offered little to the workers. The Provisional Government had the support of the Mensheviks and SRs who commanded a majority in the soviets which mushroomed during and after the February revolution.

The economic and political paralysis of the regime drove a wedge between the Provisional Government and the mass of workers, peasants and soldiers. The first crisis of the Provisional Government came in April. The issue was the war. The Cadet leader Miliukov provoked the crisis by declaring that 'Russia would fight to the last drop of her blood'. It was an announcement which met with a bitter response on the battlefields where Russian soldiers were 'churned into gruel', according to General Sir Alfred Knox, 'until casualties in the firing line should make rifles available'.[32]

Meetings, protests, street fights between pro-war and anti-war demonstrators and, eventually, riots drove Miliukov from the government. Indeed it brought an end to the purely bourgeois government. The leaders of the moderate socialists joined a new coalition government. As the Cadet Prince Trubetskoy wrote, 'There was apparently a wall between ourselves and the left, but it fell down'.[33] As the Provisional Government became progressively more unpopular it increasingly relied on the SRs and other moderate socialists to lend it credibility, ending with one such figure, Kerensky, as its leader.

The Mensheviks and the Socialist Revolutionaries were willing co-optees. They were happy to participate in the Provisional Government because they believed the revolution must limit itself to bourgeois horizons. As Trotsky notes, 'From the time of the first revolution, the Mensheviks had inferred the necessity of a union with the liberals from the bourgeois character of the revolution.'[34] The leader of the Cadets agreed:

> The socialist parties of the present time have a much more intelligent view…the revolution at the present time cannot go further than the political victory of the bourgeoisie… The socialists have even managed to break with their own traditions and doctrines and have entered the government. This represents a great step forward…[35]

This 'intelligent view', which 'systematic thinkers' like Robin

17

Blackburn and Hobsbawm now laud as showing the October revolution to be 'premature', was at the time the very theory which earned its authors the contempt of the vast majority of workers and peasants.

The moderate socialists earned this contempt by continuing policies which mirrored those of the Cadet-only government. Kerensky continued the insanity of the war effort by telling troops that 'the inevitability and necessity of sacrifice must rule the hearts of Russian soldiers' and that 'I summon you not to a feast but to death'. To which one peasant replied, 'What's the use of the peasants getting land if I'm killed and get no land?' It was an argument whose elemental power launched tens of thousands of soldiers on the long trek back to their villages. They simply walked away from the front in the summer of 1917.

At the army headquarters the supposed representatives of 'the peasants in uniform' led a rather different life from those in the barracks and trenches. Victor Serge records:

> The supreme revolutionary authority was the committee of the armies...controlled by the Socialist Revolutionary party. This committee hobnobbed amicably with the General Staff, denounced Bolshevik plots and affirmed the indefatigable loyalty of the army to the fatherland and Allies...[36]

It was no different on the home front. The Mensheviks and the Socialist Revolutionaries temporised endlessly about declaring that the land should be taken over by the peasants, despite the fact that the peasants were already acting for themselves. The Mensheviks, including Martov, were adamant in their opposition to workers' control of the factories, again in spite of the fact that this was a reality even before it became a Bolshevik slogan. But they could do nothing to stop the crisis which was driving the workers to occupy the factories and the peasants to seize the land: prices rose 2,300 percent between February and October and real wages fell by almost a half.[37] The rate of bankruptcies and closures rocketed. Strikes alone were not enough to combat this level of social disintegration.

A second crisis erupted in July as Kerensky's military offensive failed and as the Provisional Government used Czech mercenaries to drive recalled veterans to the front. The anger of the workers and soldiers spontaneously boiled over into a near uprising—'more than a demonstration and less than a revolution',

18

in Lenin's words.[38] At one point an angry mob burst into the soviet and, white with anger, a worker jumped onto the platform, shook his fist at the SR leader Chernov and shouted, 'Take power, you son of a bitch, when it's given you.'

But the SRs and Mensheviks had no intention of proclaiming, 'All Power to the Soviets.' As one historian generally unsympathetic to Bolshevism writes:

> Too long used to debating the complexities of revolutionary theory while they remained unschooled in revolutionary practice, the men who stepped forward to lead the Petrograd Soviet...proved to be timid advocates for Russia's proletarians...these halting theorists preached that the revolution neither had 'the practical strength to bring about the rapid socialistic transformation of Russia, nor were conditions ripe' for doing so. Political power, they insisted, must be delivered first to those sober politicians who represented Russia's men and women of property... Petrograd's workers and soldiers proved much less willing to surrender their newly won revolutionary victories.[39]

The immediate consequence of the July Days was not to increase the support for the Bolsheviks. The wave of the revolution had broken around the walls of the Provisional Government without yet being powerful enough to breach them. As the movement temporarily ebbed, reaction, confident that the moderate socialists were as fearful of the masses as it was, seized its chance.[40]

Just as polarisation was taking place within the soviet camp an equal but opposite polarisation was taking place in the camp of the bourgeoisie. Just as the soldiers, workers and peasants were impatient for the Provisional Government and the moderate majority in the soviets to resolve the situation decisively in their favour, so the generals, the factory owners and the landlords were losing patience with the Provisional Government's inability to resolve the situation once and for all in their favour.

Inside the bourgeois camp the mood began to swing in favour of a military dictatorship. Kerensky ordered the formation of a special squad to hunt down Lenin and shoot him on sight.[41] Trotsky and other leading Bolsheviks were imprisoned, Bolshevik sympathisers were murdered and the organisation's printing presses smashed. 'A common parlour topic became the need for an "exemplary" German victory, to chasten the working class'.[42] Marc Ferro has described what he calls this 'terror in an minor key':

> A model of anti-Bolshevism was being assembled, and it was reconstituted during the civil war. It was shaped between February and October, and there was some similarity between it and the Fascist model that came later in Italy and then Germany: it began with resistance to social revolution, the primary role of leading financiers and industrialists, with action by the army and the church, denial of the class struggle, and an appeal to servicemen's masculine solidarity; it was followed by the use of 'special action groups', the denunciation of governmental weakness, the emergence of new men (often former revolutionaries who had supported the war), with a leadership cult, anti-Semitism, attacks on democratic organisations, and finally, the sympathy and armed intervention by allied governments.[43]

The appearance of General Kornilov in Moscow for the state conference in August 1917, born aloft from his train by officers, was the turning point. From that moment on the Provisional Government became a fiction. Behind its facade the Bolsheviks prepared to defend the revolution by ending dual power in favour of the soviets. The right prepared to crush the revolution, the soviets and the Provisional Government beneath the heel of the army. The choice was either revolution or counter-revolution. Trotsky argued:

> Just as out of the eagerness of the Petrograd masses arose the semi-insurrection of July, so out of the impatience of the property owners arose the Kornilov insurrection of August. And just as the Bolsheviks found themselves obliged to take the side of an armed insurrection, in order if possible to guarantee its success and in any case to prevent its extermination, so the Cadets found themselves obliged, for like purposes, to take part in the Kornilov insurrection. Within these limits, there is an astonishing symmetry in the two situations. But inside this symmetrical framework there is a complete contrast of goals, methods and results.[44]

Kornilov was clear that he and his fellow officers 'would not hesitate to hang all the soviet members if need be', but he hoped to operate under the wing of Kerensky's government. Then a Constituent Assembly could be summoned, quickly dispersed and 'Kerensky and Co will make way for me'.[45] 'The Kornilovshchina was to begin, under the Kerenshchina's cover'.[46] Kerensky belatedly realised that Kornilov's plans would end in his own demise and turned to the soviets to defeat the Kornilov coup. The soviets, in turn, were now disillusioned with Kerensky and increasingly looked to the Bolsheviks for leadership.

So the same process which was draining popular support from the Provisional Government towards the soviets also began, within the soviets, to drain support away from the moderate socialists toward the Bolsheviks. In August 1917 the president of the Mensheviks declared that the organisation was in 'total confusion. No one knew what to do or how to proceed... The Mensheviks and the SRs were equally isolated from the people and from the soldiers.' Plekhanov's paper surveyed the work wrought by his theory that the revolution was 'premature' and concluded, 'The Menshevik faction is suffering one defeat after another, and one does not have to be a prophet to foretell rapid demise'.[47]

In these circumstances the moderate socialists lost all purchase on political reality. Continually declining in influence they were tossed back and forth between wanting to prevent a second revolution and realising that if they did not go forward they would be thrown back into the arms of counter-revolution. Kerensky's increasingly hysterical vacillations were the personification of this attitude.

The Bolsheviks' vital role in organising the defeat of the Kornilov coup gave them the support of the majority in the soviets. The Kornilov coup was defeated at the end of August and on 9 September the Bolsheviks won the majority in the Petrograd soviet, Trotsky becoming its president. Between the defeat of Kornilov and the October insurrection the task of the party was to organise its supporters in the soviets, and indeed to convince some of the party's own leaders, so that the broken hulk of the Provisional Government could be successfully deprived of the last vestiges of power.

Lenin insisted that the insurrection could only be the crowning act of the mass revolution, not a party coup. Nikolai Podvoisky, the Bolshevik head of the Petrograd soviet's Military Revolutionary Committee, recalled this conversation with Lenin on the eve of the October revolution:

Comrade Lenin asked me what I thought of the work of the Military Revolutionary Committee.

'The Military Revolutionary Committee', I answered, 'is actually an extended bureau of the Military Organisations of the Central Committee of our party.'

'And that is wrong!' said Vladimir Ilyich. 'It should not be a bureau, but a non-party insurrectionary body which has full power and is connected with all sections of the workers and soldiers. The committee must ensure that an unlimited number of workers and soldiers are armed and participate in the insurrection. The greater the initiative and activity of each member of the Military Revolutionary Committee, the stronger and more effective will be the influence of the entire committee on the masses. There must not be the slightest hint of the dictatorship by the Military Organisation over the Military Revolutionary Committee.[48]

This was, of course, not the first time Lenin had had to argue the difference between a revolution and a coup. Both the Mensheviks and some of his own supporters, notably Zinoviev and Kamenev, had objected that Lenin was planning a coup when he demanded practical military preparations for the revolution. Lenin was variously accused of Jacobinism, or of being a follower of the anarchist Bakunin or the conspirator Blanqui. Lenin's answer is worth quoting at length since it shows both that he had no intention of mounting a coup and precisely the preconditions for revolution which had been achieved by October. These same arguments were contained in his pamphlet *Marxism and Insurrection*, circulated in thousands of copies before the October revolution:

Military conspiracy is Blanquism, if it is organised not by a party of a definite class, if its organisers have not analysed the political moment in general and the international situation in particular, if the party has not on its side the sympathy of the majority of the people, as proved by objective facts, if the development of revolutionary events has not brought about a practical refutation of the conciliatory illusion of the petty bourgeoisie, if the majority of the soviet-type organs of revolutionary struggle that have been recognised as authoritative or have shown themselves to be such in practice have not been won over, if there has not matured a sentiment in the army (if in wartime) against the government that protracts the unjust war against the will of the whole people, if the slogans of the uprising (like 'All Power to the Soviets', 'land to the peasants', or 'Immediate offer of a democratic peace to all the belligerent nations'…) have not become widely popular, if the advanced workers are not sure of the desperate situation of the masses and of the support of the countryside, a support proved serious by a peasant movement or by an uprising against the landowners and the government that defends the landowners, if the country's economic situation inspires earnest hopes for a favourable solution of the crisis by peaceable and parliamentary means. That is probably enough.[49]

When Lenin believed that these conditions were *not* present, during the July Days, he bent his every effort to *prevent* a premature rising. Many other revolutionaries in Europe, as the German revolution would show, were to pay with their lives for not being able to make a similar assessment. But by October even Lenin's political enemies were forced to admit that he was no Jacobin. The Menshevik N N Sukhanov writes:

To talk about military conspiracy instead of national insurrection, when the party was followed by the overwhelming majority of the people, when the party had already de facto conquered all real power and authority—was clearly an absurdity. On the part of the *enemies* of Bolshevism it was a *malicious* absurdity, but on the part of the 'cronies' [Zinoviev, Kamenev] an aberration based on panic. Here Lenin was right…[50]

Or as Robert Service simply expresses it:

What really counted was that the Bolshevik political programme proved steadily more appealing to the mass of workers, soldiers and peasants as social turmoil and economic ruin reached a climax in late autumn. But for that there could have been no October revolution.[51]

Martov wrote, 'Understand, please, that before us after all is a victorious uprising of the proletariat—almost the entire proletariat supports Lenin and expects its social liberation from the uprising'.[52]

Ultimately October was not a great contest between Menshevism and Bolshevism, not between bourgeois democracy and soviet power but between *bourgeois reaction* and military dictatorship, on the one hand, and soviet power, on the other. The Mensheviks did not understand this at the time of the revolution, they did not understand it at the time of the dissolution of

23

the Constituent Assembly and they did not understand it during the civil war. The Bolsheviks' ability to prevail lay in the fact that they did understand this.

Those who dream today that there could have been a 'third way' which would have prevented the 'premature' revolution of October 1917 need to think on two issues. Firstly, such a course was offered to the workers of Russia in 1917 and they rejected it and, secondly, they rejected it in part because they saw behind the vacillations of Kerensky the bayonet of Kornilov. Trotsky was right when he insisted that fascism is the price paid by those who toy with revolution.

The Bolsheviks: a monolithic party?

The root of Stalinism is often said to lie in the Bolsheviks' tyrannical and undemocratic party structure. This was the mantra repeated by a generation of Cold War historians, now echoed in the Russian media. Their central argument has been summarised with only a hint of irony by liberal historian Stephen Cohen:

> In October 1917, the Bolsheviks (Communists), a small, unrepresentative, and already or embryonically totalitarian party, usurped power and thus betrayed the Russian Revolution. From that moment on, as in 1917, Soviet history was determined by the totalitarian dynamics of the Communist Party, as personified by its original leader, Lenin—monopolistic politics, ruthless tactics, ideological orthodoxy, programmatic dogmatism, disciplined leadership, and centralised bureaucratic organisation.[53]

The left used to set its face firmly against what Cohen calls this 'malignant and inevitable straight line' theory. Now, however, things have changed. Sam Farber connects Lenin's attitude to legality in the early Soviet state, which he defines as one of 'expediency at best and of contempt at worst', with 'Lenin's chronic distaste for codified rules, legal or otherwise'. This attitude, Farber claims, 'had sometimes played an important role in his political practice concerning internal party organisation'.[54] This lack of respect for 'rules' and 'legality' helped pave the way for Stalin. For Robin Blackburn, 'Lenin's Bolshevik current came to represent a species of political voluntarism'. Lenin's 'cult of party organisation and discipline' was a 'double-edged discovery' which helped 'to fashion a political force that could be used for purposes he did not approve', a fact which he only recognised at the end of his life. And although Lenin 'does not carry full responsibility' he and Trotsky 'cannot escape the charge of having themselves prepared the ground for Stalin'.[55]

These are remarkable sentiments to hear from socialists, especially since much research done by liberal historians over the last 30 years has demonstrated beyond all doubt that the Bolsheviks were, until shortly before Stalin's rise to power in 1928, an organisation who were fanatical in only one sense: their devotion to internal debate and argument.

Lenin's early insistence on discipline and organisation in *What is to be Done?* (1902) was a product of the chaos and anarchy that reigned in the revolutionary movement at that time. Local groups proliferated without contact with one another. Primitive and amateurish, prey to police agents, they were often arrested before they produced their first leaflet. The upsurge of strike activity from which they had emerged had marked them with a healthy desire to participate in the struggle but with a marked unwillingness to relate this struggle to the wider issues of socialist change within society.

The famous themes of *What is to be Done?* addressed themselves to these weaknesses. Where there were only leaflets, Lenin demanded a party press. Where there was amateurishness, Lenin demanded professionalism. Where there was syndicalism and economism, Lenin demanded socialist politics. Where there was localism, Lenin demanded coordination and centralisation. And all this itself demanded an active, not passive, membership. Illegal conditions required a high level of commitment from 'professional' revolutionaries. All these formulations from *What is to be Done?* were at the time supported by Trotsky and by Martov.

On occasions Lenin's arguments overstated the case—a necessary evil given the chaos above which he was trying to rise. It was untrue that socialism could only come to the workers 'from the outside' and it was untrue that workers could spontaneously reach only trade union consciousness—faults which Lenin was only too pleased to acknowledge three years later when he announced that workers were 'spontaneously' socialist during the 1905 revolution and that the party should open its gates wide to admit as many of them as possible.[56] Even when illegality and repression obliged the Bolsheviks to adopt tighter organisation they were far from the totalitarian organisation of legend. As one liberal historian notes:

> The image of a tightly knit bunch of inveterate conspirators, so sedulously cultivated by their enemies, was…a cruel mockery of their real condition. Indeed so much of their public reputation was wide of the mark. They did not look upon Lenin, even when he succeeded in keeping in contact with underground committees, as the only acceptable source of plans and policies. They did not regard *What is to be Done?* as an organisational blueprint…they in fact wanted to found a mass socialist party as soon as it was practicable.[57]

The Bolsheviks were so far from being a monolithic party that Lenin had enormous difficulty in getting many committees to separate from the Mensheviks at all. Even in 1917 there were still joint committees in some parts of Russia. At all points from 1905 to 1917 the Bolsheviks were a party in which heated discussion was the norm. They divided over boycotting and later participating in the Duma, over participation in the police inspired trade unions, over the philosophical dispute between Lenin and Bogdanov and over a host of lesser issues.

In 1917 itself 'controversy was the lifeblood of Central Committee activity'.[58] They were of course famously divided over the very nature of the revolution, over if and when to call for a second revolution. After the revolution they divided over whether there should be a coalition with other socialists, over whether the elections to the Constituent Assembly should be rerun and about whether there should be a peace with German imperialism. This last 'had for a time…brought the party to the edge of the abyss of total disintegration'.[59] Yet it did not prevent further arguments over military policy during the civil war, the role of trade unions under socialism and, repeatedly, over economic issues. In his study of the internal organisation of the Bolsheviks, Robert Service notes that even though the devastating experience of the civil war had sapped the inner life of the party:

> This is not to say that the Bolshevik party of the mid-1920s was yet the regimented grotesquerie it was to appear in the 1930s…with all these controversies raging throughout the 1920s

it would be ludicrous to maintain that the stuffing had been completely knocked out of Bolshevik life not long after the civil war.[60]

These arguments often split the Bolsheviks from top to bottom, as any serious argument in a revolutionary party is likely to do. At all times, but especially in 1917, 'insubordination was the rule of the day whenever lower party bodies thought questions of importance were at stake'.[61] During 1917 the Vyborg committee of the party sent out its own agitators to tour the Baltic arguing against the Petrograd committee's tolerant attitude towards the Provisional Government:

> Nor was there a well established system of subordination and discipline along the hierarchical chain stretching from the Central Committee at the apex to the primary 'cells' at the base. Tension and conflict were the rule, not the exception. If anything committees tended to be called into account from below rather than above. Rank and file members and lower activists could not only make their views known at general open meetings but also re-elect their representatives at frequent intervals… [F]ew leaders succeeded in acting in opposition to the viewpoint of their committee colleagues over a lengthy period.[62]

It was frequently the local party committees which inundated the Central Committee secretariat with demands for more precise guidelines about what they should do. Often Sverdlov, in charge of the secretariat, could only tell them to look at *Pravda* for guidance. As October approached he was unable to do more than tell one inquirer, 'You understand, comrade, that it is difficult to give you instructions any more concrete than "All Power to the Soviets" …except to add that it is of supreme importance to take charge of the post and telegraph offices and also the railway'.[63] This minimal guidance, even in Petrograd, was not always followed: both the comrades charged with leading the detachment which seized the general telegraph office forgot to bring the revolvers.

So what is left of the importance of organisation and the operation of democratic centralism if this is a true picture of how the Bolsheviks worked? Actually, a great deal. A revolutionary party operates precisely by being in a relationship of 'tension and conflict' both with the mass of the working class and with the ordinary members of the party who are subject to the pressure of the mass of workers.

Without such pressure, without the tumultuous democracy and debate which is the ordinary functioning of a revolutionary organisation, it is impossible for the party to learn what is going on in the class, to discuss and debate its own experience and to formulate policy. But without the constant attempt to rationalise and systematise its work and its arguments the party cannot act as the organ which attempts to lead the class—that is why a party must try to discipline the debate and discussion, even while it welcomes it. The only means that the leadership of the party has to achieve this is the power of argument and the record of its previous decisions. The stronger this record, the more frequently the party and its leadership have been proved right in struggle, the more weight it carries in the class and with its own rank and file. And, in the last resort, the power of the leadership's arguments will depend on how quickly and effectively it learns from workers in struggle, the only real source of theory.

The Bolsheviks could tolerate a high level of internal debate because they had, over many years, created a high level of agreement on general politics and a wide knowledge of the Marxist tradition. Equally importantly they had sought at every available opportunity to root themselves in the working class, training their members never to stand aloof from the struggle and to express the party's ideas in terms which fitted the experience of those in struggle. In contrast, Rosa Luxemburg's Spartacus League had neither a common theoretical framework nor well established links with at least an advanced minority of workers. This is why it could neither act in a concerted manner during key turning points in the struggle, nor could it withstand fierce debate without running the risk of immobilising the organisation.[64]

Once this dialectical relationship between the Bolsheviks and the working class was broken, shattered because the working class itself was broken backed after the civil war, freedom of debate gradually and inevitably became first a monologue of the party with itself and then merely a dispute among the leaders of the party.

The Constituent Assembly

The dissolution of the Constituent Assembly by the Bolsheviks in January 1918 is one of their most contentious acts. It outraged Kautsky and became one of the key accusations in *The Dictatorship of the Proletariat*, his polemic against the October revolution. Robin Blackburn is obviously sympathetic to Martov's view that the 'bourgeois democratic revolution should be championed by Marxists'. Blackburn goes on to argue that 'consistent with this position, Martov opposed dissolution of the Constituent Assembly in 1918 while still favouring an independent role for the soviets and trade unions.' Martov, says Blackburn, 'attacked the Bolsheviks for a sort of lumpen anarchism which failed to see the importance of establishing a lawful and democratic polity based on an authoritative state'.[65] Robin Blackburn isn't above bracketing Kautsky and Rosa Luxemburg together as 'notable Marxists of the day' who 'repudiated the practice of party dictatorship from the very beginning'.[66]

In an earlier issue of *New Left Review* Tim Wohlforth puts the same kind of argument in more general terms. 'It is hard to view the young Soviet state as *structurally* superior to the systems of parliamentary, "bourgeois" democracy excoriated in Leninist doctrine', argues Wohlforth. He goes on to say that soviets should be supplemented by 'the direct election by universal suffrage and secret ballot, through free competition of parties, of the highest decision-making body of government'.[67]

Sam Farber is half willing to defend the Bolsheviks, but '*only if we assume* that their arguments in defence of the soviet system …represented a genuine long-term commitment to that alternative form of democratic government'.[68] Yet this is precisely what Farber is not willing to assume since his whole book is supposed to demonstrate that the Bolsheviks failed to show any such commitment. Sam Farber too quotes Rosa Luxemburg, whose criticism of the Bolsheviks' dissolution of the Constituent Assembly is cited by right wingers who would never dream of endorsing any other word that she wrote. In particular, they forget her accolade to Lenin and Trotsky who, she said, had been 'the salvation of the honour of international socialism'.[69]

The essential problem with all these criticisms is that they ask the question: if we were the founding fathers of the workers' constitution, what democratic blueprint would we propose? The question they do *not* ask is: in the struggle for power which institutions represent the interests of the workers and which the interests of the ruling class? Around which institutions are the opposing classes rallying? These questions need careful analysis in a revolutionary period because the role of the different institutions alters dramatically depending on the balance of class forces.

Before the October revolution all the socialist parties, including the Bolsheviks, had been in favour of calling the Constituent Assembly. Yet the Provisional Government, both before and after the socialists joined it, had delayed calling the Assembly. This delay had a social root. If the elections had been held the Mensheviks and SRs would have had a majority. This would have forced them to address the land question, the ending of the war and the occupations of the factories. This would have meant that they would either have had to agree to the Bolsheviks' programme—'Land, Bread and Peace'—or they would have had to try and claw back the already half established gains of the revolution. That would have meant siding with the counter-revolution against the mass of workers and peasants.

So the Provisional Government did what it was best at: it temporised and made excuses. On the one hand it said that it could not decide the key questions of the day because it was only a *provisional* government. On the other hand it delayed calling the one body which it maintained did have such power, the Constituent Assembly. In these circumstances the Bolsheviks called all the more vociferously for the Constituent Assembly as a way of showing that the bourgeois democrats had no intention of even carrying through the tasks of the bourgeois revolution. Meanwhile, they continued to insist that the tasks of the revolution could only be met by transferring all power to the soviets.

Even before the October revolution the mass of workers understood clearly that the soviets were their organisations, responsive to their needs, and that the Assembly was a chimera of which they knew little and from which they expected less. Boris Sokolov, one of the leaders of the SRs, explains this graphically:

> Of all the political parties the Socialist Revolutionary Party was linked with the idea of the Constituent Assembly by extremely close, I might even say organic, ties... It seemed to them, and not only to them, that the crucial thing was to 'bring the country

to the Constituent Assembly'. Theoretically perhaps, and probably in fact, there was a very great truth in this, but practically this peculiar idealism was fraught with the most exasperating consequences and complications.

This was especially because the people were far from being fully imbued with faith in the saving power of the Constituent Assembly... In the beginning, during the first few months after the revolution, the Constituent Assembly was something absolutely unknown and unclear to the mass of front line soldiers...their sympathies leaned completely, openly, and frankly to the soviets. These were institutions that were near and dear to them, reminding them of village assemblies ... From the very first days, the meetings of the soviets influenced their decisions. Both the army committee, which the soldiers called 'our soviet', and the soviets in the capital cities seemed close to them, and their activities comprehensible. During the first few months I more than once had occasion to hear objections to the Constituent Assembly from soldiers, and not from the least intelligent ones at that. To most of them the Assembly was associated with the State Duma, an institution that was remote to them. 'What do we need some Constituent Assembly for when we have our soviets, where our deputies meet and which can decide everything and know how to go about everything?' [70]

After the October revolution had transferred power to the soviets, the SRs and the Mensheviks no longer wished to delay calling the Constituent Assembly for now it had been transformed from a looming embarrassment into a potential base from which they might be able to regain all that they had just lost. Again the mood was very different among the rank and file. Sokolov reports from a congress of soldiers held on the south western front, where, it should be noted, Bolshevik influence was much less than on the north western front:

A majority of the congress belonged to the SR Party, which had approximately two thirds of the delegates. The remaining third adhered to the Bolsheviks or a small number to the Ukrainians. However, some of the SRs, primarily those sent by rearguard units in the front line zone, took an ambiguous position, which could best be summed up as follows: since the Provisional Government no longer exists and since the Constitutional Assembly has not yet been convened, all the power in the country ought to go to the soviets...

The disputes that developed on this question showed how con-
tradictory the mood was even among the delegates... They
discussed the advantages of the soviet system over parliamentar-
ianism and emphasised the fact, which seemed indisputable to
most, that the soviets were better than the Provisional Government
since the 'soviets, you know, are ours'. Even the arrival of the
former Provisional Government minister Avksentiev at this congress and his many speeches in defence of the slogan 'All Power
to the Constituent Assembly', did not convince the majority...
The front line congress, though not by a very large majority,
expressed itself in favour of the formulation proposed by the
Bolsheviks. It spoke out for power to the soviets—essentially
for Bolshevik power.[71]

Thus these soldiers understood through experience what had
become, since Marx's writings on the Paris Commune, a cor-
nerstone of revolutionary theory: that the soviet is a superior form
of democracy because it unifies political and economic power—
unlike parliament which leaves the most important power of the
bourgeoisie, its economic strength, untouched; because it brings
under democratic control the administrative and legislative functions of government—unlike parliament which leaves the civil
service, army and police in unelected hands; and, most of all,
because the soviet is an organ of struggle responsive to the will
of the workers and capable of directly organising strikes, protests
and so on.

A parliament could be a rallying point for the bourgeoisie
during their revolution precisely because they aimed only at *political* power. In general they were already masters, or near masters,
of the economy. The Long Parliament of 1640 in England and the
Constituent Assembly of 1789 in France therefore restricted
themselves to conquering state power on behalf of an already
economically powerful class. Even in these cases parliamentary
institutions had to be propelled forward by, respectively, the arms
of the New Model Army and the force of the great popular mobil-
isations led by the Jacobin clubs. In both the English and the
French revolutions the most radical sections of the bourgeoisie
even had to purge their own parliamentary institutions in order
for the revolution to succeed.

But the socialist revolution must counterpose the soviet to parliament, just as the bourgeoisie counterposed parliament to the

court, precisely because it needs an organ which combines economic power—the power to strike and take control of the workplaces—with an insurrectionary bid for political power, breaking the old state and replacing it with a more democratic workers' state.

The bourgeoisie and the SRs clearly understood this and were keen to restore all the old separations inherent in a bourgeois state as the first step on the road to counter-revolution. The Constituent Assembly was a rallying point for the right. The SRs planned what was effectively a counter-revolution to coincide with the opening of the Constituent Assembly:

> Everything was ready to transform the event into an insurrection. Thirty armoured cars were to advance against the Smolny [the Bolshevik headquarters]; SR regiments would have supported the coup.[72]

'For weeks all preparations had been made with this end in view. But by the new year it was evident that a strictly military coup could not succeed,' comments Radkey, the historian of the SRs.[73] At the last moment the SR leadership called off the rising. Nevertheless the SR terrorist fraction still made plans to kidnap Lenin and Trotsky and on 2 January 1918, three days before the Assembly was due to open, two shots were fired at Lenin's car. And in southern Russia the first White 'volunteer army' under General Kaledin was already fighting soviet power under the banner of the Constituent Assembly. Under these circumstances it would have been absurd for the Bolsheviks to allow this invitation to counter-revolution to remain open, even if the elections to it had been scrupulously fair according to the lights of parliamentary democracy.

In fact they were not fair even according to those limited criteria. Firstly, the elections only achieved a 50 percent turnout and in some parts of Russia no poll was held at all. On some sections of the front, officers hid the fact that the Provisional Government had fallen. Secondly, the SRs had split after their election lists had been drawn up. This meant that the Right SRs (RSRs) who were little different to the 'left' Cadets, dominated. The Left SRs (LSRs), who were close to the Bolsheviks, only got their lists out to some of the central Russian regions.

Thus the three weeks of polling which gave a massive majority to the RSRs and about 25 percent of the votes to the Bolsheviks were highly unrepresentative of the real situation. A brief look at three of the areas where the LSRs did manage to stand candidates reveals how much the result would have altered had they been allowed to stand everywhere. In Petrograd the LSRs received 16.2 percent of the vote and the RSRs 0.5 percent; in Kazan the LSRs got 18.9 percent and the RSRs 2.1 percent; in the Baltic Fleet 26.9 percent voted for the LSRs, while just 11.9 percent voted for the RSRs.[74] Even allowing for the fact that these were favourable areas for the LSRs it is clear that the election results were a mockery of the real situation in Russia in 1917.[75] The elections to the all-Russian congresses of the soviets give a much more accurate picture of the Bolsheviks' support:[76]

CONGRESSES	NO OF DELEGATES	NO OF BOLSHEVIKS	%
1 June 1917	790	103	13
12 Oct 1917	675	343	51
3 Jan 1918	710	434	61
4 Mar 1918	1232	795	64
5 July 1918	1164	773	66

The real weakness of the bourgeoisie was symbolically represented by the scene at the dissolution of the Constituent Assembly. 'Meeting in this atmosphere of botched insurrection, the Constituent Assembly felt itself doomed', records Victor Serge.[77] Certainly when the anarchist commander of the Red Guard, to chants of, 'That's enough! That's enough!' from a packed gallery, approached the chairman and told him that the Assembly would have to disperse because 'the guard is tired', the delegates went meekly enough.

The only outcry was a small demonstration, dispersed with a few casualties by the sailors, which even Sokolov described as 'absurd, ridiculous'. Victor Serge states that, 'The dissolution of the Constituent Assembly made a great sensation abroad. In Russia, it passed almost unnoticed'.[78] And that doyen of Cold Warriors Leonard Shapiro comments, 'It was the end of the Constituent Assembly. Its dispersal caused little stir in the country and was reported to have been treated with indifference in the army'.[79] W H Chamberlin, the *Christian Science Monitor*'s Moscow correspondent in the 1920s, records in his valuable, though anti-Bolshevik, *The Russian Revolution* that the dismissal of the Constituent Assembly 'evoked scarcely a ripple of interest and protest, so far as the masses were concerned.' Even Pipes is forced to admit that 'the dissolution of the Assembly met with surprising indifference'.[80]

There can be little doubt that if the situation had been reversed, that is if a Bolshevik dominated Constituent Assembly had been elected while the right wing still commanded sufficient armed force, they would have dismissed the Assembly.

Once again the German revolution provides a negative proof of the correctness of the Bolsheviks' attitude to the Constituent Assembly. The revolution of 9 November 1918 had been won on the basis of strike action, mutiny and the rise of workers' councils. But the German soviets, like their Russian counterparts after the February revolution, were dominated by reformists. The government of People's Commissars, drawn from the reformist SPD and the centrist USPD, immediately began to argue that the soviets had done a marvellous job in getting rid of the Kaiser, but that they should now prepare to hand over power to a Constituent, or National, Assembly. This was Kautsky's repeated theme during these months.[81]

Confronted with the practical question, 'National Assembly or soviets?' Rosa Luxemburg, less than a year after she first made her criticisms of the Bolsheviks' attitude to the Constituent Assembly, immediately abandoned them. Sam Farber mentions this change of heart in a fleeting phrase, but then hurries on like a rich man avoiding a beggar. Let's halt this guilty conscience in its tracks and see what Luxemburg said. She pilloried 'the National Assembly as an attempt to assassinate both the revolution and the workers' and soldiers' councils'.[82] And her paper, *Rote Fahne*, declared:

> The National Assembly is a device with which to cheat the proletariat out of its power, paralyse its class energy, and make its final goals vanish into thin air. The alternative is to put all power into the hands of the proletariat, develop this incipient revolution into a mighty class struggle for a socialist order, and to this end establish the political supremacy of the working masses, the dictatorship of the workers' and soldiers' councils. For or against socialism, for or against the National Assembly. There is no third choice! [83]

These were prophetic phrases. In the end the reformist led

counter-revolution felt strong enough to strike without waiting for the National Assembly to be convened. But the propaganda for the Assembly had done its work in demoralising and demobilising the workers' councils. In Germany the contest of dual power was resolved in favour of the bourgeoisie, with the help of propaganda about the National Assembly. The right exacted a terrible price. Armed bands of right wing troops, the Freikorps, the swastika on their arms and the Constituent Assembly as their slogan,[84] inaugurated a reign of terror. Rosa Luxemburg, Karl Liebknecht, Leo Jogiches and Eugene Leviné, the outstanding leaders of the German revolution, were murdered. In Berlin alone 3,000 workers were slaughtered in pitched battles with the Freikorps. It was a counter-revolution planned and led by the reformist SPD. Its figurehead was SPD deputy Gustav Noske. In Noske's own words:

> Nobody made any objection when I expressed the view that order would have to be restored by force of arms. The Minister of War, Colonel Reinhardt, drafted an order appointing as commander-in-chief General Hoffmann… It was objected that this general would be too unpopular with the workers… I insisted that a decision must be taken. Somebody said: 'Perhaps you'll do the job yourself?' To this I replied, briefly and resolutely: 'I don't mind, somebody's got to be the bloodhound. I'm not afraid of the responsibility!' It was decided forthwith that the government would grant me extraordinary powers for the purpose of re-establishing order in Berlin. In his draft, Reinhardt struck out the name of Hoffmann and replaced it by mine. That is how I was appointed to the post of commander-in-chief [85]

Four days after the murder of Luxemburg and Liebknecht the elections for the National Assembly took place. When it met, the SPD formed a coalition with the two bourgeois parties. In Russia the Bolsheviks' ability to win the majority in the soviets to take power meant the crushing of the Constituent Assembly as a centre for counter-revolution, at least in the heart of Russia. Henceforth counter-revolutionary assemblies were expelled into the south and to the east of the Urals. In Germany the Spartacus League's weakness and inexperience allowed a reformist leadership of the workers' councils to crush the revolution and hand power to a bourgeois assembly.

The scale of that tragedy spread all the way from Berlin to

Petrograd and Moscow. Without a successful German revolution the Bolsheviks were thrown back into a bloody civil war with only limited resources. The revolution was under siege.

The civil war and the White Terror

The civil war was a bloody and brutal era. On many occasions the life of the Soviet regime hung by a thread. To survive at all the regime underwent a severe change which dramatically altered the elementary freedoms which the Bolsheviks, like everyone else, took for granted in the first period of Soviet power.

For many writers it was in this period of War Communism that the first seeds of Stalinism were sown. Joe Slovo argues, 'The foundation for the institutionalised separation of socialism and democracy, both in the party and in society, was laid in ideological practices which preceded the emergence of an economically privileged strata.' He cites Trotsky's writings from the period of War Communism as containing 'quite a few ideological positions which also degrade the ideas of communism'.[86] For Robin Blackburn:

> 'War Communism', with its far-reaching attempt to replace all exchange by requisitioning…cast a blight on small-scale production in this backward country. It was also associated with an intensified and hardened Bolshevik sense of destiny that would brook no opposition.[87]

Sam Farber is happy to repeat Robert C Tucker's designation of this period as 'Stalinist Leninism' and goes on to argue:

> The governmental euphoria with War Communism also implicitly revealed the political and ideological priorities of mainstream Bolshevism. Thus, while this set of policies greatly expanded the powers of the central state and vigorously attempted to reduce the role of the market, at the same time it not only consolidated the Red Terror but for all intents and purposes eliminated workers' control of industry and democracy in the soviets. Again there is no evidence indicating that Lenin or any mainstream Bolshevik leaders lamented the loss of workers' control or of democracy in the soviets…[88]

Slovo, Sam Farber and, to a lesser extent, Robin Blackburn all have a similar methodological refrain to back up this attitude. It runs like this: yes, objective conditions were bad during the civil war, but this can't explain everything. 'This simplified form of economic determinism has its limits', says Slovo.[89] There must, therefore, have been some weakness in Bolshevik theory. For Sam Farber 'ideological inebriation' among the Bolsheviks 'negates the claim that War Communism...was simply imposed on the government by objective necessity'.[90]

This sounds like sophisticated Marxism: rejecting crude economic determinism in the name of taking 'political factors' into account. But, properly used, Marxism does not suggest that in every circumstance political will or ideology can play a key role. The degree to which workers can 'make their own history' depends on the weight of objective factors bearing down on them. At the height of the revolutionary wave such freedom can be considerable. In the concentration camp it can be reduced to virtually zero.

Of course there was a point on the revolutionary front where consciousness, theory and organisation were decisive for the Bolshevik revolution at this time: that point was the European, particularly the German, revolution. But in Russia the limits of action were reduced to withstanding a siege, under ever narrowing constrictions. Every ounce of will power and political consciousness was necessary to keep the workers' state from being overcome. The 'subjective factor' was reduced to a choice between capitulation to the Whites or defending the revolution with whatever means were at hand. Within these limits Bolshevik policy was decisive. But it could not wish away the limits and start with a clean sheet. It is a tribute to the power of the Bolsheviks' politics and organisation that they took the measures necessary and withstood the siege for so long.

To decide in any given circumstance the weight of the subjective and objective factors demands a concrete analysis of the balance of forces. This is precisely what is missing in most accounts. Sam Farber cheerfully brandishes his desire to concentrate on the political, and criticises others who see 'the question of democracy as if it was in some way derivative of economics'. Presumably, in this schema, 'democracy' is equally possible under starving, plague ridden feudalism as it is under 20th century capitalism. In Sam Farber's analysis of the civil war we are blankly told that 'the atrocities carried out by the White

Terror are assumed to be given'.[91] Yet this is what *cannot* be assumed to be given. If we do not give a full account of the economic crisis, the international situation and the depth of the White Terror how can we be expected to judge how far the Bolsheviks acted from necessity? How can we assess the force of circumstance?

So what were the conditions facing the Bolsheviks? The civil war broke over a country already decimated by the First World War. By 1918 Russia was producing just 12 percent of the steel it had produced in 1913. More or less the same story emerged from every industry: iron ore had slumped to 12.3 percent of its 1913 figure; tobacco to 19 percent; sugar to 24 percent; coal to 42 percent; linen to 75 percent. The country was producing just one fortieth of the railway track it had manufactured in 1913.[92] And by January 1918 some 48 percent of the locomotives in the country were out of action.[93] Factories closed, leaving Petrograd with just a third of its former workforce by autumn 1918. Hyperinflation raged at levels only later matched in the Weimar Republic. The amount of workers' income that came from sources other than wages rose from 3.5 percent in 1913 to 38 percent in 1918— in many cases desperation drove workers to simple theft. The workers' state was as destitute as the workers: the state budget for 1918 showed income at less than half of expenditure.[94]

Starvation came hard on the heels of economic devastation. In the spring of 1918 the food ration in Moscow and Petrograd sank to just 10 percent of that needed to sustain a manual worker.[95] Now it was Chicherin, the People's Commissar for Foreign Affairs, who ironically repeated the threat first made by the millionaire Ryabushynski: 'The bony hand of hunger may throttle the Russian Revolution'.[96] Disease necessarily walked hand in hand with starvation, claiming perhaps 7 million lives during the civil war, the same number of deaths as that suffered by Russians in the First World War. The tone of this cry from Lenin testifies to the seriousness of the crisis in 1918:

> For God's sake, use the *most* energetic and *revolutionary* measures to send *grain, grain* and *more grain*!!! Otherwise, Piter [Petrograd] may perish.[97]

It was against this backcloth of economic devastation that the civil war took place. October had been a decisive turning point in the revolution, but it was far from the end of the struggle. As Chamberlin observes, 'The alternative to Bolshevism, had it failed to survive the ordeal of civil war...would not have been Chernov, opening a Constituent Assembly...but a military dictator, a Kolchak or a Denikin, riding into Moscow on a white horse'.[98]

Most historians treat the revolution and the civil war as separate processes. In reality they were one. The attempted suppression of the Bolsheviks in July 1917 and the Kornilov revolt the following month had been the precursors of civil war before the revolution. Just three days after the revolution, while the revolution itself still hung in the balance in Moscow, the workers of Petrograd were out digging trenches before the city to defend it from General Krasnov's Cossacks who, with Kerensky, had already captured Tsarskoye Selo a few miles from the capital.

The following day Colonel Polkovnikov led an insurrection of the junkers of the military school in Petrograd. They captured the central telegraph office and Commissar Antonov before they were defeated. Antonov kept his promise to ensure their safety. But the junkers did not keep their promise not to bear arms against the soviets and, as soon as they were released, threaded their way through Red territory toward the centres of White resistance in the Don and Kuban territories and in the Ukraine where White armies were already forming.

The day after the junker rising Krasnov's forces, joined by leaders of the Socialist Revolutionaries, did battle with the Reds on the Pulkovo Heights outside Petrograd. Krasnov was beaten and the Whites made their way to the south and east. Soviet power still did not exist in much of the country and the civil war never entirely died down. Fighting continued throughout the following months, especially in the Ukraine. Trotsky left his post as Commissar for Foreign Affairs to become War Commissar in March 1918. This catalogue of armed resistance to the revolution makes a nonsense of Pipes's claim that 'the Bolshevik terror' began long 'before any organised opposition to the Bolsheviks had had a chance to emerge'.[99]

Indeed, as most historians admit, the Red Terror did not begin in earnest until the late summer of 1918. But three months earlier the Bolsheviks had received a terrible lesson in terror from the Whites in Finland. Until the October revolution Finland was part of the Russian Empire, albeit with its own democratic constitution granted as result of the 1905 revolution. In 1917 Kerensky dissolved the Finnish parliament when the Social Democratic majority voted for independence. New elections gave the Social Democrats 92 out of 200 seats, but by now a revolutionary situation was developing. Russia's October revolution was greeted with a general strike in Finland. By January 1918 a Council of People's Delegates had been formed and red flags flew over the major towns. But White Guards had prepared to meet this threat and they got the support of German troops. In the brief civil war that followed the Reds were beaten, but the mass killings were revenge, committed after the event.

In Helsinki the Whites made workers' wives and children walk in front of their troops as they recaptured the city street by street. One hundred of the women and children died. In all, some 300 corpses were found in the streets. Later 40 women were laid out on the ice and shot. In Tavastehus 10,000 prisoners were interned and many died in the massacre which followed during which 'murder of the wounded was the norm.' In Kuumen 500 were shot after the battle and in Rauma another 500 were shot'.[100] In Sveaborg there were public executions and in Lahti 'in one day some 200 women were shot with explosive bullets: lumps of flesh were spattered out in all directions.' In Viipuri 600 Red Guards were lined up in three rows and machine gunned to death.[101]

> …from 28 April to 1 June the number of illegal killings was 4,745, just over half of all such killings, and the peak period from 5-11 May saw executions average 200 a day. In total the illegal killings of captured Reds, or those taken to be such, totalled 8,380, which included 58 victims under 16, and 364 women.[102]

In addition there were another 265 'legal executions', but the 'formal investigations were perfunctory' and 'the basis on which the charges were brought illegal'.[103] Nor was this the end of the White Terror. Some 80,000 were taken prisoner during May:

> they were herded into improvised prisons, often grossly overcrowded, unsanitary and lacking the most basic facilities…nobody on the winning side felt that the food shortages of the prisoners merited special consideration.[104]

In four months 11,783 prisoners died of this deliberate neglect.[105]

41

In all, the Finnish White Terror claimed the lives of 23,000 Reds.[106] It was a fate which must have burnt itself into the minds of the Bolsheviks and steeled their hearts during the civil war. Yet neither Pipes nor Sam Farber can spare as much as a sentence for the White Terror in Finland.

Imperialist intervention in Russia began to gather pace just as the White Terror was taking its vengeance on the Finnish workers. It was designed to exacerbate the economic and political crisis in Russia to the point where the Bolshevik regime cracked into pieces. The German occupation of the Ukraine meant that 80 percent of Russia's pre-war grain was now beyond the Bolsheviks' control. After the Bolsheviks signed the peace of Brest-Litovsk in March 1918, a peace which sanctioned the German occupation, they remained in control of only one seventh of Imperial Russia's sugar beet fields and only one quarter of its coal mines, iron foundries and steel mills.[107] And in 1918 the Allied blockade of Russia began. By the start of the following year 'not one letter, not one food parcel, not one package of goods, not one foreign newspaper could enter Red Russia'.[108]

In April 1918 the British and the Japanese seized Vladivostok in the east. By the end of the year there were 73,000 Japanese troops, 60,000 Czech troops, 8,000 US troops, 2,500 British troops, 1,500 Italian troops and 1,000 French troops fighting the Reds *in Siberia alone*.[109] During the course of the civil war the Bolsheviks would face armies from 14 different countries, including all the imperialist powers. From the east these would support the White forces of Kolchak as they streamed over the Urals toward Moscow. From the north the British and US forces supported the Whites as they attempted to thrust south toward Petrograd. From the south the French and others would support General Denikin and the Don and Kuban Cossacks as they drove north toward Moscow. Later the Polish would invade from the east and General Iudenich would come within a rifle shot of Petrograd. By 1919 more than 200,000 Allied troops were supporting the Whites.[110] Trotsky describes the front in August 1918 as:

> a noose that seemed to be closing tighter and tighter around Moscow... The soil itself seemed infected with panic...everything was crumbling. There was nothing left to hang onto. The situation seemed hopeless.

Not for the last time, the Bolsheviks were only in control of an area 'now reduced to the size of the ancient Moscow principality. It hardly had an army; it was surrounded by enemies on all sides'.[111]

It is often said that war imposes a terrible symmetry on its opposing sides. This is particularly true of civil war. Trotsky learnt cavalry tactics from the White Cossacks, just as Cromwell learnt them from Prince Rupert. And Trotsky, like Cromwell, surpassed his master. The Russian Civil War, fought in desperate economic conditions, imposed a particular ferocity on each side. Brutality was countered by brutality, White Terror by Red Terror. Yet inside the symmetry of war there was also a vital difference which the war highlighted: the difference in the class basis of the opposing armies. White General Krasnov described his own army's composition:

> Not more than half were fit for combat. The remainder were priests, nurses, miscellaneous females, officers of the counter-intelligence services, policemen, aged colonels who had signed up as commanders of non-existent regiments and, finally, various 'personalities', all of them with a more or less colourful past, who were in search of positions as governors, vice-governors, and mayors.[112]

As General Iudenich's troops advanced on Petrograd from the north 'old officials, old landlords, old policemen were apt to follow in their wake', one observer noted.[113] And in the early stages of the civil war when General Denikin captured Ekaterinodar one Cadet exclaimed, 'There are our gendarmes, yes, indeed our old, pre-revolutionary gendarmes'.[114] After his retreat from Ekaterinodar, General Denikin found himself in charge of a force approaching 4,000 of whom 2,368 had been officers, including 36 generals and 200 colonels. Another 1,036 had been sergeants or corporals.[115]

The US ambassador to Japan reported that 'the Kolchak government has failed to command the confidence of anybody in Siberia except a small discredited group of reactionaries, monarchists and former military officials.' This is unsurprising given the Siberian government's view that 'it is impossible to abolish capitalist forms of industry… Capitalist forms of industry must exist, and capitalists as a class must be allowed to direct them'.[116] And of course everywhere and always the arrival of the Whites meant that the old landlords tried to regain their land and to return to the age old rule of the knout.

Given the social composition of the Whites' leading circles and the frankly counter-revolutionary programme on which they acted it is no surprise to find that although terror was used by both sides it was used most completely, with far greater barbarity, bloodshed and loss of life by the Whites. This was an absolute necessity for the Whites since they were unable to win the support of the population with anything like the success that the Bolsheviks achieved. In those areas controlled by the Whites the pretence of democratic government, where it existed in the first place, was quickly abandoned. Both in the Ukraine and in Siberia the short lived Constituent Assemblies quickly handed power to military dictatorships. Serge observed:

> Point for point, the experience of the Ukraine, where democratic parties of the middle class could do nothing except open the path for black reaction, is repeated in Siberia. Such, indeed, is the inevitable function of these parties in civil wars, since the peculiarity of the bourgeoisie is to have no politics of its own. It is always situated between two dictatorships, that of the proletariat, or that of reaction; its destiny is to prepare the latter, up to a certain point, and then to submit to it.[117]

Soon, everywhere that the Whites ruled, dictatorships of a kind only later rivalled by the Nazis held sway. 'The greater the terror, the greater our victories', declared Kornilov. 'We must save Russia', he argued, 'even if we have to set fire to half of it and shed the blood of three fourths of all the Russians!'[118] It was clear to the Bolsheviks what such declarations meant from the time, early in the civil war, when the Whites loaded three freight cars with corpses and marked them: 'Fresh meat, destination Petrograd'.[119]

When the Whites retook Kiev in August 1919, 'anti-Semitic venom fairly dripped from some of the public pronouncements of Denikin's generals.' One of these vowed that 'the diabolical force that lives in the heart of the Jew-Communists will be destroyed'.[120] W Bruce Lincoln, not a pro-Bolshevik historian, writes that Denikin:

> imposed a regime marked by...a vicious hatred for all Jews. As the pogroms of 1919 burst upon the Jews of the Ukraine with an

incredible ferocity, the enemies of Bolshevism committed some of the most brutal acts of persecution in the modern history of the Western world.[121]

In these pogroms the 'identification of the Jews with the Bolsheviks played a central part':

No longer spontaneous outpourings of racial and religious hatred, pogroms now became coldly calculated incidents of wholesale rape, extreme brutality and unprecedented destruction. In a single day at the end of August in the Jewish settlement of Kremenchug, the Whites raped 350 women, including pregnant women, women who had just given birth and even women who were dying.[122]

In Kiev, the anti-semitic Cadet Shulgin remembers, 'gigantic five and six storey buildings began to shriek from top to bottom'.[123] In the town of Felshin a third of the Jewish population perished. In 1919 alone, just in the Ukraine, the Whites killed 150,000 Jews, a rate only exceeded by the Nazi Holocaust. One in 13 of the Jewish population of the Ukraine had been slaughtered.[124]

In Kolchak's Siberia the same methods held sway. Even the Cadet Nikolai Ustrialov described it as 'the darkest, most mindless sort of military reaction…the rearguard of a past that is slipping into eternity'.[125] Under Kolchak's jurisdiction was Ataman Semyenov: 'Innocent men and women dangled by the scores from telegraph poles in the vicinity of his capital, and his men machine-gunned freight cars full of victims at execution fields along the railway'.[126] Also fighting alongside Kolchak was Ivan Kalmykov, who Baron Budberg, one of Kolchak's own officials, described as 'a sadistic bandit' and 'a fully qualified war criminal'.

By the orders of another White leader, Baron Urgan-Sternberg, 'men and women suffered death by beating, hanging, beheading, disembowelling and countless other tortures which transformed them from living human beings into what one witness called a "formless bloody mass".' Even his own staff physician described one of the Baron's written orders as 'the product of the diseased brain of a pervert and a megalomaniac affected with a thirst for human blood'.[127] Admiral Kolchack himself, when some members of the executive of his government suggested there should be some reforms, 'pounded the table with his fists, flung everything on the floor, seized a penknife, and angrily slashed the arms of the chair' before replying:

45

Leave me in peace. I forbid you to bring up such questions. Today I am going to the council of ministers and will order that…there will be absolutely no reforms.[128]

For the troops of Kuban Cossack General Shkuro, a conservative historian has written, 'The chief inducement offered them was loot, for Shkuro was not particular where he looted or how…if he had to kill people he preferred that they should be Bolsheviks'.[129] Meanwhile, also in the Kuban:

Cadets…looked on while reactionary General Dragomirov began the persecution of Jews that would turn into full-fledged pogroms…and the sadistic General Pokrovski hanged socialists en masse in the courtyard outside his window 'to improve the appetite'.[130]

General Mai-Maevsky, a veteran of Denikin's army, 'was capable of the greatest cruelty, and had a penchant for orgies'.[131] Denikin's successor, Wrangel, describes one of his own senior officers, General Slaschev, as 'thoroughly addicted to narcotics and alcohol'. On visiting Slaschev's quarters Wrangel found him sprawled in a jumble of liquor bottles wearing a fantastical uniform made from a long white Turkish robe trimmed with gold and fur. 'There was', Wrangel says:

a crane and a raven, a swallow and also a starling…fluttering here and there and perching on their master's head and shoulders… I was dealing with a man completely overcome with mental illness.[132]

The whole existence of the White camp—its social composition, its policies, its methods and the character of its leading figures—is utterly at odds with the social profile of the Reds. Unless these vital differences are understood it becomes impossible to explain how the Bolsheviks won the civil war. Again and again we find that even the Whites themselves admit the vital difference between their regime and the Reds. An official report to Kolchak's War Ministry, detailing the state of one of its armies in 1919, says:

Ataman Krasilnikov is completely inactive, devotes himself exclusively to drinking and disorderly conduct; his officers act in the same way: the soldiers carry out arbitrary searches with the purpose of robbery and violate women. The whole population is eager for Bolshevism. The situation is critical.[133]

In Siberia, reported US General Graves, 'the word Bolshevik meant a human being who did not...give encouragement to the restoration to power...of autocracy in Russia.' He went on to assert that 'outside the office holding and military class, the Omsk [Kolchak] government had less than 1 percent of followers'.[134] The Cadet Ustrialov reported that in Omsk the 'poor openly rejoice and wait for the Bolsheviks to arrive'.[135]

It was more or less the same story in other White areas. In the Northern territory, the SR Boris Sokolov records, 'the sentiment of the population of Archangel and of the villages have convinced me that the majority of the population is in sympathy with the Bolsheviki'.[136] Another supporter of the northern White government admitted that 'the mass of the people is turning back to Bolshevism'.[137] And of Denikin's regime in the south, Chamberlin says:

> With all its shortcomings, the Soviet regime was popular with the masses of the *inogorodni* [outlanders, non-Cossack peasants with limited rights], who feared, with good reason, that the return to power of the Cossack Rada [parliament] would mean not only the end of their dreams of confiscating some of the more abundant possessions of the Cossacks, but also a period of very sanguinary revenge and repression.[138]

Denikin himself describes his own governors:

> In psychology, world outlook and habits they were so alien to the upheaval that had taken place that they could neither understand it nor deal with it. For them everything was in the past and they attempted to resurrect this past in form and spirit. After them followed the minor agents of the old regime, some of them terrified by the Revolution, others embittered and revengeful.[139]

Chamberlin acknowledges that in the last instance it was Denikin's lack of popular support 'which was the fundamental cause of the defeat of the Whites'.[140]

Besides the different attitude of the Bolsheviks to the workers and the peasants there was another vital difference with the social policy of the Whites which helped ensure a Red victory: the attitude to the rights of nations to self determination. The Whites of course were unremittingly hostile to any such right. Their constantly proclaimed slogan was, 'Russia shall be Great, United and Undivided.' The great Russian chauvinism of the Whites made it inevitable that they should take such a position, despite the fact that it was to prove fatal to their cause.

In the north west 'the stubborn unwillingness of the Whites, obsessed with the idea of a "great undivided Russia", to recognise the independence of Finland and Estonia, the cooperation of which would have been very desirable in operations against Petrograd, was a not inconsiderable cause of their defeat'.[141]

The White army of western Russia, headed by General Count Rudiger von der Goltz, was:

> notorious for its brutal treatment of Latvians, Estonians and Bolsheviks. Called by some the 'vanguard of Nazism' the Freikorps units...instituted what one British diplomat called a 'veritable reign of terror' that claimed the lives of some 3,000 Latvians in Riga alone.[142]

In the south:

> It was Denikin's misfortune that much of the population in the territory under his control was non-Russian and that his prospects of military victory depended very much on his ability to conciliate Ukrainians and Poles, Georgians and Caucasian tribesmen; a task for which he was completely unfitted...[143]

In fact Denikin forbade teaching of the Ukrainian language.

With such disaffection among the population of the White areas it is little surprise to find that a similar attitude often developed among the rank and file of the White armies, whether they were indigenous Russians or foreign interventionists. Of course there were many cases of desertion and passing over to the Whites in the Red Army. But the scale was greater among the White troops. In north Russia in 1919 nearly half of the White troops, some 6,000 men, went over to the Reds in two weeks when their commander gave them the choice. Whole regiments went over en masse. At about the same time British and French units in the area mutinied and one US sergeant recorded in his diary:

> The majority of people here are in sympathy with the Bolo [ie Bolsheviks]. I don't blame them, in fact I am nine tenths Bolo myself.[144]

One Red officer, risking his life, deserted to Kolchak. But he was so disgusted at the all pervasive indiscipline and debauchery that he drew a sharp comparison with the Red Army where, he said, an intoxicated officer would have been shot by the first commissar who met him. Chamberlin concludes:

> Not all the Communists, certainly, were saints or puritans. But their general behaviour and morale seem to have been better than those of their opponents.[145]

Towards the end of the Kolchak regime, even the dictator's personal bodyguards drew the same conclusion: when Kolchak gave them a free choice about whether they should continue to follow him or join the Bolsheviks, 'almost to a man, the men in whose loyalty he had believed absolutely repaid his trust by joining the Bolsheviks'.[146] Such was the decomposition of the White camp at the end of the civil war. But in order to achieve this victory the Bolsheviks had to make, and had to demand that the mass of peasants and workers make, the most costly of sacrifices.

War Communism and the Red Terror

In 1918 the economic wreckage in the country, the constant pressure of foreign intervention and blockade and the terrifying ferocity of the White Terror meant that the sacrifices necessary to win the civil war would not be made, or could not be made in time, simply through the normal methods of political debate.

When SRs assassinated leading Bolsheviks simply to rely on political re-education to convince them of their error was an act of suicide. While the Whites held a gun to the peasant's head and a bayonet to his child's throat no amount of political propaganda alone would convince the peasant to defy the Whites. When the imperialist armies pressed towards Moscow conscription was a necessity since there simply was not the time for a disciplined, extensive, fully politically conscious, armed population to have been organised to meet them. Ten years breathing space could have created such an armed population, but the Bolsheviks' time scale was measured in weeks. When the cities starved it would have been better to bring the peasant to give grain to the regime in return for the far greater gift of machinery—but for that revolution in Germany, or at least the revival of industry, was necessary. In the absence of both all that stood between the workers' state and its destruction at the hands of Kolchak and Denikin was grain requisitioning.

49

This dialectic of consent and coercion is, of course, an aspect of any workers' revolution. More than 30 years ago Tony Cliff put it like this:

> Under capitalism discipline confronts that worker as an external coercive power, which capital has over him. Under socialism discipline will be the result of consciousness, it will become the habit of free people. In the transition period it will be the outcome of the two elements—consciousness and coercion. Collective ownership of the means of production by the workers, ie the ownership by the workers' state of the means of production, will be the basis for the conscious element in labour discipline. At the same time the working class as a collective, through its institutions—soviets, trade unions, etc—will appear as a coercive power as regards the disciplining of the individual workers in production.
>
> This conflict between the individual and the collective, the necessity of uniting conviction with its ugly opposite, coercion, the compulsion on the working class to use barbaric methods remaining from capitalism to fight capitalist barbarism, is but another affirmation that the workers are not liberated spiritually under capitalism, and would take a whole historical period to grow to full human stature.[147]

In a country where the working class was a minority of the population, where industry had been battered by years of war and in conditions of White and imperialist encirclement, the balance gradually tilted towards greater coercion. Each step of the way was forced on the Bolsheviks by dire and pressing necessities. Every element of coercion was an emergency measure adopted for the simple reason that the only other alternative was the triumph of counter-revolution. It was the realisation of this fact which ensured that even while many workers and peasants bridled under the regime of War Communism they fought to the death to defend it from the Whites. It is also why the most draconian forms of coercion intertwined with the most conspicuous acts of heroism in every aspect of the War Communist regime.

In the economic field the Bolsheviks' immediate steps after the October revolution were modest. They did not want wholesale nationalisation and were content to gradually try and regularise a situation where the workers' control in the factory coerced and cajoled the existing owners. As S A Smith writes in

Red Petrograd, his detailed study of workers' control in the factories:

> This awkward fact makes a nonsense of the claim in Western historiography that, once power was in his grasp, Lenin, the stop-at-nothing centraliser, proceeded to crush the 'syndicalist' factory committees.[148]

Of course the fact that workers now controlled the state machine meant that they had a powerful tool with which to circumscribe the limits within which the jostling development of mixed companies would take place. The local factory committees were the first to call for the power of the workers' state to be used to structure industry. They above all realised that workers' control in the factory must be complemented by workers' control over the whole economy. Indeed immediately after the revolution the All Russian Council of Factory Committees passed a decree which demanded a central apparatus to regulate the economy—it was Lenin's decree on workers' control which toned down this demand.[149]

A similar urge to put an end to the anarchy which prevailed as a result of competition between different labour organisations can be seen in the debate on the role of trade unions. The absorption of the factory committees by the trade unions is often portrayed as a Bolshevik plot to undermine the committees. In fact it was a part of the desire of rank and file militants to rationalise the mass of organisations that had sprouted during the revolution and to overcome the inherent localism of the committees. At the First All Russian Congress of Trade Unions there were only six votes against merging the committees with the unions. Both the Bolsheviks and the Mensheviks voted for merger.[150] And the Petrograd factory committees, at their sixth and final conference in January 1918, agreed to merger. Their incorporation into the unions helped to broaden the functions of the unions, giving them a role in supervising production as part of a committee in each factory.[151]

All these are perfectly healthy debates about how a workers' state is to organise its economy. At this point the economic structure is still a long way from the wholesale state control which was rapidly to be forced on the regime. The need for a breathing space, for the revolution to gather its forces, was at the heart of this strategy of state regulated capitalism which Lenin advocated immediately after the revolution. Two overwhelmingly powerful forces obliged the Bolsheviks to abandon this 'reformist' course.

One was the fact that the capitalists used their remaining power to make the system unworkable. At the end of 1917 the All Russian Congress of Employers declared that those 'factories in which the control is exercised by means of active interference in the administration will be closed'.[152] The workers' natural response to the wave of lockouts which followed was to demand that their state nationalise the factories. So it was that, of all the individual firms nationalised by July 1918, only one fifth had been nationalised on the initiative of the state while four fifths had been nationalised on the initiative of local committees.[153] But the power of the Russian capitalists alone would not have been sufficient to blow the regime off course if it had not been for a second factor: the start of the civil war and the allied intervention. One economic historian explains the impact of the armed threat:

> In the atmosphere of the kindling civil war every joint effort of capital and the proletarian dictatorship (workers' control, mixed joint stock companies etc) is seen to be a quickly evaporating Utopia.
>
> The intervention of world capital, which fanned the expiring counter-revolutionary resistance within Russia into a new blaze, forced its consequences onto the proletariat—the inexorable expropriation of large scale capital and capital generally, the confiscation of the property of the ruling classes, the suppression of the market and the construction of an all-embracing proletarian organisation of political economy, which depended on overcoming the market, and its exploitation.[154]

So, far from being an example of inherently undemocratic Bolshevik politics, as Sam Farber and others maintain, the nationalisations of War Communism were an ad hoc measure which sharply departed from the far slower, more measured path that the Bolsheviks would have preferred to tread. In fact the nationalisation of all heavy industry and joint stock companies in June 1918 was a hastily prepared measure designed to circumvent the condition of the Brest-Litovsk treaty which required compensation to be paid to German investors whose firms were not nationalised by 1 July.[155] Bruce Lincoln summarises the work of the Bolsheviks' Supreme Council of National Economy as 'reflecting little coherent planning'. Its decisions were only internally generated in a minority of cases:

> Far more often the Supreme Council worked to prevent factories being shut down by anti-Bolshevik managers or to offset crudely conceived local seizures… At best the Supreme Council's first attempts to nationalise Russia's industries reflected the Bolsheviks' overwhelming concern for self defence and survival.[156]

The Bolshevik leader Milyutin wrote, 'The process of nationalisation went on from below, and the soviet leaders could not keep up with it, could not take things in hand, in spite of the fact that many orders were issued which forbade local organisations to enact nationalisations by themselves'.[157] Lenin recognised the enormous strain that the nationalisation policy was placing on the workers' state. In April 1918 he declared, 'If we go on expropriating capital at this rate, we shall infallibly be beaten'.[158]

Yet the harder the Whites and the imperialists pressed on the regime, the more unavoidable a siege economy became. With the civil war came the need for stricter labour discipline and for the committees which ran the factories to be replaced by 'one man management'. Both these processes developed in lock step with the war. In 1919 only 10.8 percent of firms in Russia were under one man management. This figure rose swiftly during the following year. But even so, in Petrograd in 1920, only 31 percent of factories employing more than 200 were under one man management.[159] Labour discipline also tightened during the civil war, but as S A Smith records:

> During 1918 the desire to transform relations of authority within the enterprise gave way to the drive for greater productivity… Yet one cannot see in this a triumph of the Bolshevik Party over the factory committees. From the first, the committees had been committed both to maintaining production and to democratising factory life, but the condition of industry was such that these two objectives now conflicted with one another. The factory committees, in general, consented to the prioritisation of productivity: they acquiesced in, and even initiated, impulses toward stricter labour discipline.[160]

In the towns and cities workers accepted, albeit not happily, the rigours of War Communism as necessary to defend the revolution. But beyond the towns the peasants were a different problem. In the country food requisitioning—the taking of the peasants' grain, often by force—became essential to ward off the spectre of starvation. Food requisitioning was an act of desperation not, as Sam Farber argues, a dogmatic attempt to 'suppress the market'. The Bolsheviks would far rather have avoided it, if for no other reason than it threatened to split the alliance between the workers and the peasants on which the whole edifice of the state rested. As Tsiurupa, the People's Commissar of Food Supplies, put it:

> There are only two possibilities, either we perish from hunger, or we weaken the [peasant economy] to some extent, but [manage to] get out of our temporary difficulties.[161]

The Bolsheviks would have preferred the solution to the peasant question opened up by the perspective of permanent revolution: to use the industrial strength of the cities to improve the productivity of the peasants and wed them to the rule of the working class. This was also the plea from the peasants, encapsulated by peasant delegates at the Eighth Congress of Soviets in 1920:

> 'If you want us to sow all the land…just give us salt and iron. I shall not say anything more'. We need horses, wheels, harrows, other voices chimed in. Give us metal to mend our tools and sheds.[162]

It was a simple request, but under the conditions of civil war and without revolution in Europe it was a request which the Bolsheviks could not satisfy. The only other alternative was to take grain by sending out requisitioning and roadblock units from the towns. The cry for grain came from the towns and cities, as the desperate telegrams flooding into the People's Commissariat for Food Supply in 1918 testify:

WE HAVE NO BREAD. THE SITUATION IS HOPELESS. HUNGER REIGNS.—19 May, from the village of Pokrov.

IAROSLAV PROVINCE IS IN AN ABSOLUTELY UN-PRECEDENTED IMPOVERISHED AND CATASTROPHIC CONDITION SO FAR AS FOOD SUPPLIES ARE CONC-ERNED. ABSOLUTELY NO SHIPMENTS OF GRAIN HAVE ARRIVED FOR TWO WEEKS.—24 May, from the provincial capital of Iaroslav.

> STARVING WORKERS ARE COLLAPSING AT THEIR
> MACHINES... WE BEG YOU TO SEND US BREAD... THIS
> IS NOT A THREAT BUT A FINAL CRY OF DESPAIR.—25
> May, from the town of Vyksa.[163]

There can be no better testimony to the desperation that lay behind this policy than Lenin's call of July 1918 when he urged the workers of Petrograd to go 'in their tens of thousands to the Urals, the Volga and the south', insisting that it was 'criminal' and 'stupid' to sit and starve in empty factories. It was a galling necessity that the very class base of the revolution had to be consciously dispersed in order to avoid death by starvation. By September 1918 the Petrograd labour force had fallen to just below 30 percent of its 1917 figure.[164] It was a high risk policy. The countryside was aflame with peasant revolts and the food detachments were likely to be ambushed and killed. But as one official of the Food Commissariat exclaimed:

> What do you think, the People's Commissariat of Food Supply
> does this for its own satisfaction? No, we do it because there is not
> enough food. [165]

The grain was certainly there: 'Kulak [rich peasant] storehouses in the Bolsheviks' shrunken domains at midsummer [1918] still contained three quarters of a million tons of grain from the 1917 harvest plus a great deal more from earlier years'.[166]

To make the requisitioning policy work it was also necessary to highlight the difference between the village poor and the richer peasants. The former were more likely to stand by the workers than were the latter. In the short run the Committees of Poor Peasants organised by the Bolsheviks split the united front of the village into two hostile camps and therefore aided the food detachments. But ultimately they fell victim to the success of the Bolsheviks' redistribution of the land. This reduced the number of very wealthy peasants *and* the number of poor peasants, thus recomposing the united front of the peasantry. By the end of the civil war the policy of requisitioning was worn threadbare: the New Economic Policy was a recognition that the relations between the peasantry and the workers' state had to find a new footing.

Both wholesale nationalisation and requisitioning were

retreats forced on the Bolsheviks by circumstance. It is part of the Bolsheviks' achievement that they recognised the necessity and met it face to face.

Occasionally, however, they were inclined to make a virtue of necessity, to claim that the harsh measures of the civil war were the epitome of socialism. This is in part understandable; any policy must have a rhetorical power if its necessity is to be understood by millions. But what is required of historians, particularly Marxists, is to separate phrase from substance. Yet this is precisely what Sam Farber and Robin Blackburn fail to do. Instead they take Lenin or Trotsky's shouts of command in the midst of battle and portray them as considered analyses of events.

The Red Army, more than any other institution of the civil war years, embodied the contradiction between the political consciousness and circumstantial coercion. On the one hand the creation of the Red Army was a retreat: it was a conscripted, not a voluntary, army; officers were appointed not elected; old Tsarist officers were appointed by the thousand; there was severe military discipline, including execution; there was desertion and atrocities, sometimes committed by whole units. But the Red Army was also filled with a magnificent socialist consciousness. Conscription may have been necessary to build a mass army in a peasant country, but it was the most active and class conscious workers (above all the Bolsheviks) who volunteered again and again for the most dangerous tasks. In 1919 thousands deserted the party rather than fight Denikin, but thousands more joined during 'party weeks' when, as the Central Committee bulletin put it, 'to get out a party card in such conditions, signified, to a certain extent, becoming a candidate for Denikin's gallows.' In the 1920 dash towards Warsaw the Red Army lost 33 percent of its force in casualties—but some 90 percent of the army's 'hardened Bolsheviks' lost their lives.[167]

Red Army discipline was harsh, but it was harshest of all for the officers and commissars. Ordinary soldiers who returned to the Red Army after desertion would often be sworn back in; the commissars of units that deserted were frequently shot. For the White Cossack cavalry looting, rape and murder were a way of life. Looting was forbidden in the Red Army. Anti-Semitism and pogroms were rife in the White armies; anti-Semitic publications were banned in the Red Army. Pogromists were shot. In the Ukraine whole Jewish communities lived behind the Red Army lines, advancing when it advanced, retreating when it retreated.

Who can imagine the White Army reproducing the literacy and educational groups of the Red Army? Who can see the White Cossacks putting letterboards on the backs of the first rank of cavalry so that those behind could learn to read as they were on the march? And who can see the White Army producing anything like this Red Army marching song:

Two days of study, then a week in battle,
Two days with pencils, a week with bayonets.[168]

The differences between the two armies were not lost on the peasants. In the south they nicknamed the White Army the 'Grabarmiia', the looting army. In both the south and east the population came to prefer the regular exactions of the Reds to the riotous pillaging of the Whites. The difference in the class programme of the Whites and Reds decisively affected both the support which the population gave to each side and the morale of the Red and White armies. Many peasants certainly resented the grain requisitioning policies of the Bolsheviks and they often rose in revolt against them—but they did not hate requisitioning as deeply as they hated the idea that the land itself would be repossessed by the old landlords. Red troops certainly carried out atrocities, but they were not the *policy* of the Red commanders as they were of the Whites. The Bolsheviks' social policy gave other grounds for winning the trust of workers and peasants whereas the Whites had to rely on force alone. The Red Terror was certainly brutal, but unlike the White Terror it was not directed against the mass of workers and peasants in the name of a tiny and discredited old order. In the cities the Reds enjoyed the fierce and virtually undivided loyalty of the masses throughout the civil war period.

If the Red Army typified the contradictions of the civil war, the Red Terror pushed those contradictions to extremes. Of course any workers' revolution would need force to subdue counter-revolutionary risings and sabotage carried out by the old capitalist class and the remnants of its state. It was against these people that the Red Terror was directed in the first instance. As Chamberlin observes:

White Russia also had its terror, its all-pervading espionage, its frequent executions, its crowded prisons. The chief difference was in the types of people whom one would have found in the prisons of Moscow and Petrograd, on the one side, and of Omsk and Rostov on the other. The Cheka directed its raids mainly against the wealthy and the middle classes. The White police rounded up more workers and people of the poorer classes.[169]

One immediate cause of the Red Terror was the various counter-revolutionary plots mounted by Russian Whites and supported by the imperialist powers. R H Bruce Lockhart, the British diplomatic representative in Moscow, for instance, had been instrumental in ensuring that Kerensky escaped from Russia after his unsuccessful military attempt to unseat the Bolsheviks. Bruce Lockhart was also, by his own admission, passing money to anti-Bolshevik groups. Sidney Reilly, a British intelligence agent, was trying, unsuccessfully, to convince Lockhart that he 'might be able to stage a counter-revolution in Moscow'.[170] But, according to Reilly, one part of his plan was prematurely put into effect in August 1918: Socialist Revolutionary Fanny Kaplan shot Lenin twice at point blank range, bringing him close to death. Earlier Reilly had managed to establish himself as a Soviet official with access to documents from Trotsky's Foreign Ministry. And another British agent, George Hill, became a military adviser to Trotsky.[171] Overall, the British secret service:

> devoted the largest single part of its budget to Russia... It sent its best agents—fluent Russian speakers with a long experience of the country and its people—to Moscow and Petrograd with a virtually free hand to establish networks, finance counter-revolutionaries, and to do all in their power to crush the Bolshevik menace in its infancy.[172]

But the Red Terror also ran beyond these groups. The ultimate cause of the extent of Red Terror lies, once again, in the isolation of the Russian working class. The sea of peasants were the element in which the counter-revolution swam. The SRs, who claimed to represent the peasantry, were the foremost promoters of counter-revolution behind Red lines. And it was the poverty of the revolution which obliged it to use force rather than finance against the peasants who hoarded grain in the countryside.

The Bolsheviks were faced with attempts at assassination and counter-revolution such as those mounted by the (SR supported) military cadets, two days after they had been released on parole following their capture in the Winter Palace, and by the SRs at the time of the dispersion of the Constituent Assembly. Lenin never tried to hide or disguise the fact that the revolution would have to use terror, up to and including shooting people. In the struggle between revolution and counter-revolution people on both sides were willing to die for their cause: prison, let alone parole, would not deter many counter-revolutionaries:

> How can one make a revolution without firing squads? Do you think you will be able to deal with your enemies by laying down your arms? What other means of repression do you have? Imprisonment? No one attaches any importance to this during a civil war when each side hopes to win.[173]

In this Lenin was following the example of the French Revolution which, also under the impact of foreign invasion and counter-revolutionary pressure from the peasantry, used terror to ensure its existence during its darkest hour. And in 1848 Marx, in reaction to 'the cannibalism of the counter-revolution', argued that there was 'only one means to curtail, simplify and localise the bloody agony of the old society and the birth pangs of the new, only one means—the revolutionary terror'.[174]

In December 1917 the Soviet formed the All-Russian Extraordinary Commission to fight Counter-Revolution and Sabotage, known by its Russian acronym as the Cheka or Vecheka. The Cheka was only one element in the Red Terror, and not necessarily the most important part. The Red Army, the grain requisitioning and road block detachments were more important. Neither was the Cheka a specifically Bolshevik proposal. It grew out of a number of investigative commissions of the Soviet and out of the Military Revolutionary Committee of the Soviet which had carried out the insurrection. George Leggett, the intensely right wing historian of the Cheka, records:

> There is no direct evidence that the Bolshevik Party...played any part in the creation of the Vecheka; perhaps this is indicative of the relative lack of importance attached at that moment to the hasty improvisation of yet another investigative commission.[175]

It was a common understanding among all those in the revolutionary camp that the revolutionary terror was necessary, although they might argue about specific measures. The formation of the Cheka was quite open: it was announced in the

Soviet's newspaper, *Izvestia*, along with its office address, its opening hours and an appeal to the public to help combat counter-revolution. For a period it produced the *Vecheka Weekly Bulletin* in which the commission's activities, including the names of those it shot, were publicly discussed. Bruce Lockhart was taken on the Cheka's first raid as a public witness.[176] In its early days the Cheka had a small staff and its head, the Bolshevik Felix Dzerzhinsky, could carry all its files around in his briefcase.[177]

The Left Socialist Revolutionaries played a prominent role in the Cheka both during and after their time as part of the Soviet government—they left the government in March 1918 in protest at the Brest-Litovsk treaty. But it was the actions of the LSRs, alongside the worsening civil war and the mounting imperialist intervention, that precipitated a sharpening of the Red Terror.

The spring and summer of 1918 was a time of crisis for the workers' state. In April, as we have seen, the White Terror began in Finland. The Germans occupied the Ukraine following the Brest-Litovsk treaty. Some 200 Kulak revolts flared through the countryside. In June People's Commissar Volodarsky was murdered. In August Uritsky, the head of the Petrograd Cheka, was killed by a Socialist Revolutionary. In the midst of this crisis, in July 1918, the Fifth All-Russian Congress of Soviets met. The LSRs chose this moment to announce that their opposition to the Brest-Litovsk treaty was now going to take the form of armed conflict with the Bolsheviks. Their leader, Maria Spiridonova, appeared at the Congress and announced the party's return to its terrorist traditions with the instruction to 'take up the revolver and the hand grenade'. The next day she followed her own advice and appeared at the Congress brandishing a Browning and crying 'Long live the revolt!' [178]

The LSR revolt took place simultaneously in Iaroslav and other towns. It coincided with the the revolt of the commander of the eastern front at Simbirsk. In Moscow the LSRs used their base in the Cheka to execute their plans. Iakov Bliumkin, the LSR head of Cheka counter-espionage, forged Dzerzhinsky's signature on a pass, gained access to the German diplomatic representative in Moscow and shot him, hoping to smash the Brest-Litovsk treaty and provoke a new war with Germany. Bliumkin then fled to the barracks of the Cheka Combat Detachment, who were sympathetic to the LSRs. When Dzerzhinsky, with great heroism but not much tactical sense, arrived and demanded that Bliumkin be handed over, the commander arrested Dzerzhinsky. Another Bolshevik Cheka leader, Latsis, was arrested by the LSRs *inside* the Cheka head office.

The day after Uritsky was murdered, Lenin was shot by Socialist Revolutionary Fanny Kaplan. Although he was seriously wounded he couldn't be taken to hospital for fear that the surgeon would have LSR sympathies. Lenin recovered and the LSR revolt was suppressed, but the siege atmosphere in the revolutionary camp was heightened. Spiridonova, who claimed full responsibility for the revolt, was given a one year jail sentence and an immediate amnesty because of her previous 'services to the revolution'. Elsewhere the Red Terror reached a peak of ferocity. In Kronstadt the sailors and the Cheka killed 400 in a single night. In Iaroslavl, one of the seats of revolt, 200 were killed. On a single day, 3 October, 200 killings were reported in various parts of the country. Although Lenin was wholeheartedly in favour of the terror, he tried to limit the ferocity which resulted from the anger over the LSR revolt and the attempt on his life. Bruce Lockhart himself records that:

> The whole situation seemed hopeless until Lenin was able to take a hand in affairs. After he recovered consciousness, his first remark, it was said, was 'Stop the Terror'.[179]

Certainly the terror rarely assumed the popular, nationwide intensity that it reached in the period after the attempt on Lenin's life. Yet it is from this period that many right wing historians draw their most lurid stories of Cheka atrocities. Let us examine three which frequently recur. The first concerns the question of torture. A letter from a provincial branch of the Cheka, published in the Cheka paper in October 1918, demands to know, 'Why are you so soft?' Referring to the arrest of Bruce Lockhart it demands that he should be subject to 'the most refined tortures' and then sent to 'the other world'.[180] We are less frequently told that the Bolshevik Central Committee immediately upbraided the editorial board and closed the bulletin and that the Soviet, while defending the terror, renewed its condemnation of torture.[181]

The point is not that units of the Cheka never used torture, although the most extreme examples (scalping of victims, driving rats down a heated pipe held against the victim's stomach until the rat gnawed its way through the flesh) come almost exclusively from White literature—Denikin's Commission on the

Cheka and RSR leader Chernov's materials—as even Leggett admits.[182] The point is that the leadership of the Bolshevik Party, the Soviet and the Cheka itself tried to stamp it out whenever it became known. Soviet law forbade torture. Lenin defended the terror and the Cheka, but he was ruthless in punishing any abuse of its power:

> He was concerned to establish, in each case that came to his attention, whether the arrest had been necessary on purely pragmatic security grounds. Why had the Kotelnichi Cheka arrested the teacher Lubnin? Why had the Vecheka not released Kiril Semenovich Ginsburg, despite assurances given by two party members? Why had the Samara Provincial Cheka arrested the members of an expedition of irrigation experts to Turkestan? Had the food confiscation detachments and the Cavrilovo-Posadnaia Cheka acted correctly in confiscating grain? Could not Viktor Ivanovich Dobrovolskii, under arrest in Petrograd, be released? He was said to be ill, apolitical, and his family's only breadwinner... On 20 May 1919 Lenin telegraphed to the Novgorod Soviet, with a copy to the local Cheka: 'It appears that Bulatov was arrested for putting a complaint to me. I warn you that for this I shall arrest the chairman of the Cheka and the chairman and members of executive committee, and I shall press for their execution. Why did you not reply at the time to my enquiry?[183]

The second issue is the prison regime under the Red Terror. It is a standard claim of the right wing, perhaps most famously made in Solzhenitsyn's *The Gulag Archipelago*, that the prisons and concentration camps of War Communism led directly to the gulag of Stalin's day. The first and most obvious objection to this is the question of numbers: under Stalin *millions* disappeared into the camps, but even at the height of the civil war there were less than 100,000, including ordinary criminals, in the prison system. The Cheka itself had 56 camps with a holding capacity of just 24,750 in 1922. The following year the number of camps had been halved.[184] Solzhenitsyn suggests that the low numbers are a result of mass executions. Certainly there were some such executions of prisoners, although they were not Cheka policy and the most serious were in direct contravention of Cheka orders.[185] In the White areas there were few camps for the simple reason that mass execution was the policy, contrary to Pipes's ridiculous claim that 'the White armies...never elevated terror to the status of policy'.[186] In the White controlled Don of Krasnov and Kaledin, for instance, Order No 2428 read:

> It is forbidden to arrest workers. The orders are to hang or shoot them.

Order No 2431 elaborated:

> The orders are to hang all arrested workers in the street. The bodies are to be exhibited for three days.[187]

Not only was the *extent* of the prison system utterly different under War Communism from how it was under Stalin, so was its *nature*. The systematic degradation and torture of prisoners, so powerfully recounted by Solzhenitsyn, was not, as he maintains, a feature of the pre-Stalin period. The 1924 Corrective Labour Code stated:

> The regimen should be devoid of any trace of cruel or abusive treatment, the following by no means permitted: handcuffs, punishment cells, solitary confinement, denial of food, keeping prisoners behind bars during conversations with visitors.[188]

Medvedev argues that 'in most cases this code was observed at the time' and that although 'in the early 1920s there were quite a few instances that could be classified as insulting treatment of prisoners...this was the exception, not the rule'.[189] Indeed the Bolsheviks insisted that prisoners received the same food as those outside, poor though it was. Prisoners were allowed freedom of speech and of the press. They often produced their own journals which expressed views hostile to the government. In Irkutsk prisoners produced *Thought Behind Bars*, in Vitebsk, Omsk and elsewhere *Prisoner's Thought* appeared and in Kharkov, Penza and other places *The Prisoner's Voice* was published.[190] Needless to say not a trace of this regime was to survive into the Stalin years. In any case, the Bolsheviks were clear that the prison regime was a product of the civil war. A Cheka decree of January 1921 read:

> The prisons are filled to overflowing, not with bourgeois but for the most part with workers and peasants [involved in theft or speculation]. This legacy [of the civil war] must be done away with; the prisons must be emptied and we must carefully see to it that only those who are really dangerous to the Soviet regime should be put there.[191]

IN DEFENCE OF OCTOBER

The third example often used by right wing historians is based on Cheka leader Latsis's 1918 claim that whether a suspect was a capitalist or a worker was enough to determine their guilt or innocence. He went on to urge, 'Don't search the records for whether someone's revolt against the Soviet was an armed or only a verbal one'.[192] Sam Farber quotes Latsis, but does not bother to quote Lenin's angry rebuttal in which he said that 'one need not go to the same absurd lengths as Comrade Latsis.' Lenin went on to insist that Latsis 'wanted to say that Red Terror meant the forcible suppression of exploiters who attempted to restore their rule, but instead he put it this way... "Don't search(!!?) the records for evidence of whether his revolt against the Soviet was an armed or only a verbal one".'[193]

Nor was this attitude peculiar to Lenin. Dzerzhinsky himself personified the high ideals at which the Cheka aimed. He had spent a third of his life in prison for his political beliefs and he ruthlessly punished Chekists who were guilty of abuses. He insisted that Chekists must have 'a cool head, a warm heart and clean hands'.[194] Dzerzhinsky's integrity was irreproachable: he angrily turned away a fellow worker who tried to give him bacon and potatoes during the terrible days of Russia's famine. The burden of his work weighed heavily on his shoulders. On the eve of 1919, during the worst days of the terror, he turned to his fellow Bolsheviks saying:

> I have spilt so much blood that I no longer have any right to live. You must shoot me now.[195]

The same mood seized many other Chekists. Bukharin once said:

> Do not let us forget how many of them who remain are nervous wrecks, and sometimes hopelessly ill. For their work was such torture, demanding such enormous concentration, it was so hellish, that it called for a truly iron character.[196]

Of course not all Chekists possessed this 'iron character'. Some abused their power. Some tortured, imprisoned and executed unjustly. Latsis, his outburst noted above notwithstanding, could, like Dzerzhinsky, show understanding of the complexity of the Cheka's task. He insisted that to stop the power of the Cheka corrupting its members they should meet three criteria: they should be a party member, they should have a high degree of personal integrity and they should not stay long in the service of the Cheka.[197] Rotation of staff was partially implemented and many Bolsheviks spent at least some time in the Cheka.

Are these mere anecdotal or biographical details? No, they speak of the very nature of the regime. Among the Whites corruption and utterly indiscriminate terror ran from top to bottom of the regime; indeed, as we have seen, in many cases the senior commanders were personally responsible for some of the worst atrocities. With the Bolsheviks the atrocities ran against the nature of the regime and once the necessity of the Red Terror could be dispensed with the Bolsheviks moved swiftly to curtail it. Even while the civil war raged the role of the Cheka was restricted once the periods of immediate danger were past. Leggett notes:

> In the inevitable clash between the arbitrary violence of the Cheka and the system of Soviet law evolved by the People's Commissariat for Justice, the Cheka gained the upper hand whenever the regime came under threat; when the crises receded, the [People's Commissariat] won the advantage.[198]

And Latsis himself argued that the Cheka:

> has no place in our constitutional system. The time of civil war, the time of extraordinary conditions of existence of Soviet power, will pass, and the Cheka will become superfluous.[199]

But the longer the civil war lasted, the more declassed the proletariat became, the more relations with the peasantry worsened, the more the Cheka grew and the worse the quality of its members became. Latsis noted that 'unworthy elements, sometimes even counter-revolutionaries, attached themselves to the Vecheka, some for motives of personal gain'.[200] Serge observed the 'rapid effects' of 'professional degeneration' among the Chekists and recorded that 'Dzerzhinsky himself judged them to be "half rotten", and saw no solution to the evil except in shooting the worst Chekists and abolishing the death penalty as soon as possible'.[201]

The Bolsheviks moved to dismantle the Cheka as soon as the civil war was over. In 1921 Dzerzhinsky made his own proposals for the reform of the Cheka. Kamanev believed they did not go far enough and wrote to Lenin with his own proposal:

1. Relieve the Cheka of everything except political crimes, espionage, banditry, security of railroads and stores. Nothing more. The rest to go to the NKIu [People's Commissariat of Justice].
2. The Cheka's investigative apparatus to be merged with the NKIu...[202]

Lenin replied:

Comrade Kamenev! My position is closer to yours than to Dzerzhinsky's. I advise you not to give way, and to raise [the issue] in the Politburo. Then we shall make a stand for the very maximum. In addition we shall make the NKIu responsible for any failure to report to the Politburo...on the Vecheka's defects and errors.[203]

In February 1922 the Soviet government abolished the Cheka and replaced it with a new force, the GPU. The Cheka's extraordinary powers were not transferred to the GPU. It could only deal with political cases, it had no power to sentence and it had no power to execute. Even its powers of search and arrest were more tightly defined than those of modern Britain's Special Branch. Any arrested person had to be told of the charge against him within 14 days and sent to trial or released within eight weeks.[204] Of course, even when these reforms worked fully they left intact institutions which had been brutalised by the experience of civil war. Yet it was only later in the 1920s, as Stalin's hand closed around the throat of the revolution, that the GPU became the terrorist organ of a new bureaucratic ruling class:

The reconstruction of the Cheka-GPU went on for some years in the first half of the 1920s. But it slowed down after the deaths of Lenin and Dzerzhinsky; indeed things started moving in an entirely different direction. The GPU gradually began to resume the functions that were appropriate only for a period of civil war. Under pressure from Stalin, a punitive organisation reappeared, with the right to put people in jail and camps, to exile them to remote places, and later even to shoot them without any judicial procedure, simply as an administrative act.[205]

When, in 1930, one of Stalin's victims told his interrogator that his methods would have been impossible in Dzerzhinsky's day, the interrogator laughed, 'You've found someone to remember! Dzerzhinsky— that's a bygone stage in our revolution'.[206] And

Bukharin, shortly before his own execution in 1938, observed:

> Dzerzhinsky is gone; the remarkable traditions of the Cheka have gradually faded into the past, when the revolutionary idea guided all its actions.[207]

Peasant rebellion, Kronstadt and the crisis of War Communism

The Bolsheviks won the civil war, but only at enormous cost. After the First World War the country was battered and bloodied, large sections of its industry were ruined and agriculture was severely disorganised. After the civil war the situation was far worse. Travelling in Russia in 1920 H G Wells saw only 'a vast irreparable breakdown'.[208] The Central Committee for Labour Conscription reported:

> The workers of the towns and some of the villages choke in the throes of hunger. The railroads barely crawl. The houses are crumbling. The towns are full of refuse. Epidemics spread and death strikes to the right and left. Industry is ruined.[209]

None of this was an exaggeration. *Pravda* reported that there were 17 cartloads of rubbish piled up in *every house* in Petrograd because it had not been collected during the civil war. In the depopulated streets of the revolution's first city grass and flowers broke through the paving stones. In 1921 *Pravda* reported that 25 million were suffering from famine. In the country people dug up buried horses and ate the flesh. In some areas cannibalism was the only alternative to death. 'Everyday life was prehistoric,' said Ilia Ehrenburg, 'the everyday life of the cave age'.[210] One Russian economist of the 1920s wrote: 'Such a decline in the productive forces...of an enormous society of a hundred million is unprecedented in human history'.[211] Perhaps nothing conveys the poverty of Russia more vividly than the fact that average income in Russia was nearly 20 percent *less* than that of Britain in 1688. And that was in 1913; after the civil war the proportion must have been much lower.[212]

The White and imperialist armies had of course directly caused much of the damage. The workers' state was cut off from cotton until 1920, from Baltic flax and Baku oil until late 1919, and from iron and coal from the Ukraine until 1920. The economic blockade by the imperialist powers was only lifted in 1920. And the war effort had eaten up much of what remained of industry. The Bolsheviks, said the critic Viktor Shklovski, 'ruined whole factories to make boots out of [machine] fan belts'.[213] In Russia as a whole the size of the working class was more than halved. In the major cities the proportion of workers fell even more dramatically. In February 1921 *Pravda* announced a 'severe defeat on the labour front'. Sixty four of the largest factories in Petrograd were forced to close for lack of fuel. Among them was the Putilov works, the cradle of the revolution.[214]

In mid-1920 the Polish army invaded Russia from the west and the last White army in European Russia, headed by General Wrangel, drove north from the Crimea. In the midst of this crisis rebellion swept the countryside once again. Requisitioning was still in force, despite the poor harvest of 1920. Two of the peasant revolts from 1920 and 1921 have acquired political significance: Antonov's 'Green' revolt in the province of Tambov, and Makhno's revolt in the Ukraine. For Sam Farber the Reds' response to these rebellions 'which were socially and politically quite different from the White rebellions' was based in part 'on a monstrous and schematic mockery of Marxist class analysis' which affected the revolution's 'internal strength and ability to resist the logic of Stalinist politics'.[215]

In fact the Tambov and Ukrainian risings gained popular support for precisely the same reason as the White rebellions: the peasantry's opposition to grain requisitioning. Of course the White rebellions were headed by the personnel of the Tsarist old order while the Tambov and Ukrainian risings were not. Yet the only possible beneficiaries of any success that the peasant rebellions might have had against the Reds would be the Whites: there is no question that either Antonov or Makhno had either support outside limited geographical areas or an articulated political programme of their own. Indeed Antonov had backed Wrangel, as his fellow SRs had backed the Whites throughout the civil war (although they distanced themselves from Antonov's revolt). The SR influenced Union of Working Peasantry in the densely wooded, intensely rural Tambov region had vowed to 'fight the Bolsheviks to the end'.[216]

And the methods used by Makhno and Antonov in their fight against the Red Army often mirrored those used by the Whites.

Bolsheviks caught by the Tambov Greens were nailed to trees, a single railroad spike driven through their left hand and foot lifting them a few feet above the ground. Bruce Lincoln writes:

> The Greens maimed and mutilated their victims, flaying some, quartering others, and disembowelling still others…[they] gouged out eyes, chopped off limbs, mutilated sexual organs, slashed tendons…unravelled intestines…often buried captured enemies alive, but took care to leave their victims' heads above ground so that peasant women could urinate on them before the village dogs closed in to gnaw the still living flesh from their faces and skulls.[217]

In response, the Red Army 'at first alternated between wholesale cruelty, in which they burned whole villages…and extreme leniency in which they pardoned prisoners en masse'.[218] Later mass shootings became more widespread as the Red Army became bogged down in a guerrilla battle with an enemy little different from the mass of peasants who sheltered them. Characteristically, Sam Farber mentions the shootings but not the pardons, the Red Terror but not the Green Terror.

Makhno's smaller rebellion in the Ukraine is distinguished from the Tambov rising only by the muddled anarchism of its leader. Makhno's relations with the Bolsheviks were chequered, reflecting the fast changing military situation in the Ukraine throughout the civil war. The revolution released Makhno from prison and, with Lenin and Sverdlov's help, he returned to the Ukraine in July 1918 while it was still under German puppet ruler Hetman Skoropadsky. Makhno organised a partisan Insurgent Army to fight Skoropadsky and sided with the Red Army when it marched against the Whites in December 1918. Cooperation continued until June 1919 when the Insurgent Army broke from the Red Army: 'As soon as Makhno left the front he and his associates began to organise new partisan detachments in the Bolsheviks' rear, which subsequently attacked strongholds, troops, police, trains and food collectors'.[219]

Denikin's advance against Makhno's territory in autumn 1919 quickly forced a renewal of the treaty with the Bolsheviks. Makhno harassed Denikin's troops from the rear, making their advance more difficult. But by the end of 1919 the immediate White threat was removed. Makhno refused to move his troops to the Polish front to meet the imminent invasion and hostilities with the Red Army began again on an even more widespread scale. The entries in the diary of Makhno's wife betray the nature of the movement in this period:

> February 23, 1920—Our men seized Bolshevik agents, who were shot.
>
> February 25, 1920—Moved to Maiorovo. Caught three agents for the collection of grain there. Shot them.
>
> March 14, 1920—Today we moved into Velikaya Mikhailovka, killed here one Communist.[220]

Reports from the Soviet Ukrainian Front give the same picture:

> June 18—Makhno carried out a raid on the station at Grishno, held out there three hours, shot fourteen captured officials of the Soviet and workers' organisations, destroyed the telegraph communication and robbed the food warehouse of the railroad workers.
>
> July 26—Bursting into Konstantinograd County, Makhno in the course of two days cut down 84 Red Army soldiers.
>
> August 16—having seized Mirgorod for a day and a half Makhno's followers robbed all the warehouses of the county food committee, destroyed the buildings of the Soviet and workers' organisations, smashed 15 telegraph machines, killed 21 workers and Red soldiers.[221]

These actions were consistent with an earlier resolution of the Insurgent Army which declared that it was 'the actions of the Bolshevik regime which cause a real danger to the worker-peasant revolution.' In fact it was Makhno's actions against the Red Army which made 'a brief return of the Whites possible'.[222] General Wrangel attacked while Makhno's forces were fighting the Red Army: 'As Wrangel advanced...Makhno retreated north...leaving behind small partisan units in the villages and towns to carry out covert destruction of the Bolshevik administrative apparatus and supply bases'.[223] These activities were so effective that White Colonel Noga reported to headquarters that Makhno was crucial to Wrangel's advance.[224] Indeed Wrangel approached Makhno for a formal alliance and although this was turned down Makhno did not fight with the Reds again until October 1920 when Wrangel advanced on Makhno's base. It was, unsurprisingly, a treaty of convenience on the part of both sides and as soon as Wrangel was defeated at the end of the year the

Red Army fought Makhno until he gave up the struggle and crossed the Dniester river into Romania in August 1921.

Could Makhno have provided a libertarian alternative to the Bolsheviks? The answer lies in the nature of the Makhno movement. Firstly, the movement never had any real support from the working class. Neither was it particularly interested in developing a programme which would appeal to workers. Paul Avrich, the sympathetic historian of the anarchists, writes that Makhno:

> failed to win over more than a minority of workers, for unlike the farmers and artisans of the village, who were independent producers accustomed to managing their own affairs, factory hands and miners operated as interdependent parts of a complicated industrial machine... He never understood the complexities of the urban economy, nor did he care to understand them.[225]

Makhno's advice to workers aimed at reproducing the petit-bourgeois patterns of the countryside—he told railway workers in Aleksandrovsk who had not been paid for many weeks that they should simply charge passengers a fair price and so generate their own wages.[226] In the countryside of course such politics could have greater appeal. But even here any attempt to go beyond the traditional peasant economy was doomed. Makhno's memoirs admit that 'the mass of the people did not go over' to his peasant communes, which only involved a few hundred families.[227] The real basis of Makhno's support was not his anarchism, but his opposition to grain requisitioning and his determination not to disturb the peasant economy:

> Makhno had not put an end to the agricultural inequalities. His aim was to avoid conflicts with the villages and to maintain a sort of united front of the entire peasantry.[228]

In 1919 the local Bolshevik authorities made mistakes which played into Makhno's hands: despite Lenin's advice they were dismissive of Ukrainian nationalism and they tried to carry through socialisation of the land, rather than handing it over to the peasants. But by spring 1920 they had reversed the policy towards the peasants and instituted Committees of Poor Peasants. These 'hurt Makhno...his heart became hardened and he sometimes ordered executions'.[229] This policy helped the Bolshevik ascendancy.

It is hardly surprising, given this social base, that much of Makhno's libertarianism amounted to little more than paper decrees.

71

On paper the officers of the Insurgent Army were elected—in practice the most senior commanders were appointed by Makhno.[230] One
resolution adopted at a meeting of the partisans gives the flavour of
the movement: 'To obey the orders of the commanders if the commanders are sober enough to give them'.[231] In theory Makhno's was
a volunteer army. In reality 'he was compelled to inaugurate a form
of conscription in order to replenish his forces'.[232] Makhno held
elections, but no parties were allowed to participate in them. Papers
could be published, but the Bolshevik and Left Socialist
Revolutionary press were not allowed to call for revolution.[233]
Makhno was quick to denounce the Soviet 'institutions of violence,
such as your Commissariats and Chekas', but 'Makhno's private
Cheka…quickly disposed of anyone who was suspected of plotting
against his life'.[234] Makhno's army actually had two security forces,
the Cheka-like Razvedka and the Punitive Commission, which
'appears to have been headed by Makhno's wife'.[235] Their activities
were far from negligible:

> Makhno's later campaigns are among the most bloody and vin-
> dictive in history, and in the circumstances we can safely assume
> that these [security] services were responsible for frequent injus-
> tices and atrocities. Volin [Makhno's close associate] is witness to
> the fact that they were under no effective control.[236]

When a Bolshevik cell, which included a divisional commander, was discovered in the Insurgent Army, the Bolsheviks were
denied an open trial and summarily shot by Makhno's Razvedka.[237]

Neither Makhno's social programme nor his political regime
could provide an alternative to the Bolsheviks. Even his military tactics could only be effective in limited circumstances and
only then so long as they did not disturb the age old class structure of the countryside. Ultimately his anarchism was a thin
veneer on peasant rebellion.

The rising in Kronstadt in March 1921 had essentially the
same root as the peasant rebellions. Although it was preceded by
a wave of serious but quickly resolved strikes, the motivation of
the Kronstadt rebellion was much closer to that of the peasantry
than it was to dissatisfaction among what remained of the urban
working class. Kronstadt had, of course, been a stronghold of the
revolution in 1917—but in 1921 it was strongly influenced by the
mood of the peasantry. There are several interlocking reasons
why it became prey to the mood sweeping the countryside.

Firstly, the composition of the garrison had changed. In September and October 1920 the writer and Bolshevik Party lecturer Ieronymus Yasinsky went to Kronstadt to lecture to 400 naval recruits. They were 'straight from the plough'. And he was shocked to find that many, 'including a few party members, were politically illiterate, worlds removed from the highly politicised veteran Kronstadt sailors who had deeply impressed him'. Yasinsky worried that those 'steeled in the revolutionary fire' would be replaced by 'inexperienced, freshly mobilised young sailors'.[238]

By December 1920 only 1,313 recruits of the type interviewed by Yasinsky had arrived in the Baltic Fleet (out of a planned total of 10,384). We do not know how many more new recruits arrived in the three months before Kronstadt erupted in March 1921. But we do know about the composition of some other units based at Kronstadt, like the 2,500 Ukrainians of the 160th Rifle Regiment, recruited from areas particularly friendly to the Makhno guerrillas and with less than 2 percent of Bolsheviks in its ranks.[239]

Further evidence of the changing class composition of the garrison can be gleaned from the breakdown of the social background of the Bolsheviks at the base. In September 1920, six months before the revolt, the Bolsheviks had 4,435 members at Kronstadt. Some 50 percent of these were peasants, 40 percent were workers and 10 percent were intellectuals.[240] The same figures for the Bolshevik Party as a whole in 1921 are: 28.7 percent peasants, 41 percent workers and 30.8 percent white collar workers and others.[241] Thus the percentage of peasants in the party in Kronstadt was considerably higher than nationally. It was also higher than the already unusually high percentage of peasants among the members who had joined the party in 1921.[242] If we assume that the Bolshevik Party was more working class in composition than the Kronstadt base as a whole, then it seems likely that the peasants had increased their weight in Kronstadt, as Trotsky suggested.

Sam Farber argues that the new peasant recruits would not have been enough to alter the mood of the other sailors. He criticises the Trotskyist tradition in general, and Chris Harman's *How the Revolution was Lost* in particular, for arguing that 'Kronstadt in 1920 was not Kronstadt of 1917. The class composition of its sailors had changed'.[243] But even if, for the sake of argument, we accept Sam Farber's interpretation of the evidence (and he does not look at the figures for the composition of the Bolsheviks) his point only has any validity if we take the statistics in isolation. But in reality this change in composition acted on a fleet whose ties with the peasantry had recently been strengthened in other ways. In particular, the Kronstadt sailors had recently been granted leave for the first time since the civil war. Many returned to their villages and came face to face with the condition of the countryside and the trials of the peasantry faced with food detachments. Stepan Petrichenko, the leader of the Kronstadt rising, returned to his native Ukraine between April and the autumn of 1920. He found that:

> When we returned home our parents asked us why we fought for the oppressors. That set us thinking.[244]

In fact Petrichenko became so embittered that he tried to join the Whites, and was only turned away because of his previous brief membership of the Communist Party.[245] Many other sailors had similar experiences to Petrichenko when they returned to the villages, as the hundreds of letters to the Complaints Bureau of the Baltic Fleet testify. Here is part of just one from a sailor of the *Petropavlovsk*, the battleship at the heart of the rebellion:

> Ours is an ordinary peasant farm, neither Kulak nor parasitical; yet when I and my brother return from serving the Soviet republic people will sneer at our wrecked farm and say: 'What did you serve for? What has the Soviet republic given you?'[246]

Desertions began to spiral and leave was cancelled. 'By 1921 the fleet was falling apart as an organised military force'.[247] It was the fleet's links with the peasantry which provided the bedrock for the rebellion, but other factors exacerbated the situation. The ideology of the Kronstadt garrison was one factor. Even in its heroic days the garrison had an ultra-left air. Many Kronstadters had sided with the left communists at the time of Brest-Litovsk, a number of them had joined the LSRs uprising in the summer of 1918. They had opposed food requisitioning in 1918 and were fierce opponents of Red Army type discipline.[248]

Another factor in the rebellion was the decline of the Bolsheviks' influence in Kronstadt. Many of the best Bolshevik militants of 1917 had fallen during the civil war and in the six months before the rising the party lost half its members at the garrison.

When the revolt broke the sailors took over the battleships and garrison. It was clear from the start that the accumulated pressure would allow no easy solutions. Indeed, in Petrograd Zinoviev had already essentially withdrawn the most detested aspects of War Communism in response to the strikes. The Kronstadt sailors' response was contained in their *What We Are Fighting For*:

> There is no middle ground in the struggle against the Communists…
> They give the appearance of making concessions: in Petrograd
> province roadblock detachments have been removed and 10 million
> gold roubles have been allotted for the purchase of foodstuffs… But
> one must not be deceived… No, there can be no middle ground.
> Victory or death![249]

The Kronstadters' insistence that they were fighting for a 'third revolution', freedom of expression and for 'soviets without parties' has convinced many historians that this revolt was fundamentally distinct from the White rebellions. But one must be careful to analyse exactly the difference between the conscious aims of the rebels and the possible outcome of their actions. The Bolshevik regime still rested on the shattered remnants of the working class. The Kronstadt sailors' appeals to the Petrograd workers had met with little or no response. The sailors represented the exasperation of the peasantry with the War Communist regime, but Kronstadt had no nationwide organisation and no other peasant insurrection reproduced the Kronstadters' demands.

Had the Kronstadters' demands for 'soviets without parties' been realised they would have expressed the ferocious, elemental hostility of the peasants to the Bolsheviks in particular and to the cities in general. Yet in the wake of the fall of the Bolsheviks it would not have been the moderate socialists who took power. They were in any case weaker than the Bolsheviks and where they had tried to govern in the non-Bolshevik areas they had, time and again, succumbed to (and often aided) military dictatorships. The Whites, even though their armies had been beaten in the field, were still not finished—as the emigre response to the Kronstadt rising shows. In the vacuum which would have followed the fall of the Bolsheviks, the Whites were the only remaining political force which could have profited. This may not have been the aim of the Kronstadt rebellion but, given its utopian programme and its class root, this would have been its outcome.

The Whites sensed this immediately. They had predicted a rising in Kronstadt and the White National Centre abroad strained might and main to provide food for the Kronstadters, raising a total of nearly 1 million French francs, 2 million Finnish marks, £5,000, $25,000 and 900 tons of flour in just two weeks. Indeed the National Centre was already making plans for the forces of the French navy and those of General Wrangel, who still commanded 70,000 men in Turkey, to land in Kronstadt if the revolt were to succeed.[250] As it became clear that the revolt was isolated Petrichenko was forced to come to terms with the reality of the balance of class forces. On 13 March Petrichenko wired David Grimm, the chief agent of the National Centre and General Wrangel's official representative in Finland, for help in gaining food. On 16 March Petrichenko accepted an offer of help from Baron P V Vilkin, an associate of Grimm's whom 'the Bolsheviks rightly called a White agent'.[251] None of the aid reached the garrison before it was crushed, but the tide of events was pushing the sailors into the arms of the Whites, just as the latter had always suspected it would.

After the revolt was crushed, the link between the leaders of the rebellion and the Whites became even more marked. Paul Avrich, the historian sympathetic to the Kronstadt rising, says there is 'undeniable evidence' that the leadership of the rebellion came to an agreement with the Whites after they had been crushed and that 'one cannot rule out the possibility that this was the continuation of a longstanding relationship'.[252] Petrichenko himself got in touch with Wrangel, once more using Grimm as an intermediary. He joined forces with Wrangel, recruiting sailors to join an underground counter-revolutionary fighting organisation in Petrograd. Petrichenko further suggested to Wrangel that he make use of the slogan, 'Soviets without parties', but only as a 'convenient political manoeuvre'. Once the Bolsheviks were beaten 'the slogan would be shelved and a temporary military dictatorship installed.' The balance of class forces had finally brought ideology and reality into alignment.[253]

The Bolsheviks had no choice but to crush the revolt. Had they waited, the ice in the Gulf of Finland would have melted, allowing the battleships to attack Petrograd. The battle to take the garrison was bloody, especially for the Bolsheviks. As they made their way across the ice, the guns of the battleships and the island fortresses cut them down in interlocking fields of fire. Hundreds of Red Army soldiers disappeared through holes in the ice. The death toll was 600 Kronstadt sailors, including those shot after the base was captured, and at least 10,000 Reds, including 15 of the 320 delegates from the Bolshevik Party's Tenth Congress who had joined the assault. It was, as Trotsky said, a tragic necessity.

The end of War Communism would have come whether or not Kronstadt had revolted. But the revolt made it absolutely clear the era was over. 'The Kronstadt events were like a flash of lightning which threw more glare upon reality than anything else', said Lenin.[254] The Tenth Party Congress adopted the New Economic Policy (NEP) which ended grain requisitioning. Lenin told the Congress: 'Only an agreement with the peasantry can save the socialist revolution until the revolution has occurred in other countries'.[255] The NEP was a retreat from War Communism which itself had been a retreat from the policies adopted immediately after the October revolution. The longer the revolution remained isolated and the more desperate the economic conditions in Russia, the more the retreat would necessarily become severe and dangerous.

The rise of Stalinism

The civil war had reduced industry to rubble. The working class base of the workers' state, mobilised time and again to defeat the Whites, the rock on which Bolshevik power stood, had disintegrated. The Bolsheviks survived three years of civil war and wars of intervention, but only at the cost of reducing the working class to an atomised, individualised mass, a fraction of its former size, and no longer able to exercise the collective power that it had done in 1917. Lenin wrote:

> The industrial proletariat...owing to the war and to the desperate poverty and ruin, has become declassed...dislodged from its class groove, and has ceased to exist as a proletariat... It has sometimes figured in statistics, but it has not held together economically.[256]

The bureaucracy of the workers' state was left suspended in mid-air, its class base eroded and demoralised. Such conditions could not help but have an effect on the machinery of the state and organisation of the Bolshevik Party.

The Bolsheviks' monopoly of political power had been established by virtue of the simple fact that, one by one, the parties who

77

opposed them passed over to the camp of armed counter-revolution. The Cadets had, of course, been hand in glove with Kornilov even before the October revolution and were the mainstay of every White dictatorship which surfaced during the civil war. The Right Socialist Revolutionaries had planned armed counter-revolution at the time of the dispersal of the Constituent Assembly and had become indistinguishable from the Cadets during the course of the civil war. The Left Socialist Revolutionaries had been part of the Soviet government in 1918 and remained a legal opposition until, in the summer of that year, they attempted to overthrow the government in an armed coup.

The Mensheviks were different. They vacillated. Some Mensheviks, and some LSRs, split and joined the Bolsheviks. Some joined the Whites. The rest alternated between accepting the legitimacy of the government and agitating for its overthrow. The Bolsheviks treated them accordingly. The Mensheviks were legalised or extended greater freedom during those periods when they accepted the October revolution and suppressed during those periods when they vowed to return to a pre-October regime. As E H Carr notes:

> If it was true that the Bolshevik regime was not prepared after the first few months to tolerate an organised opposition, it was equally true that no opposition was prepared to remain within legal limits. The premise of the dictatorship was common to both sides of the argument.[257]

The vice-like pressure of the civil war had transformed the state in other ways. The weight of the bureaucracy, of the army, of the Cheka, had grown enormously during the civil war. Without these institutions the October regime would have been swept away in a bloody, reactionary counter-revolution. With them the October revolution had become sclerotic and authoritarian. There were so many 'horrifying facts about drunkenness, debauchery, corruption, robbery and irresponsible behaviour of many party members that one's hair simply stands on end', one Central Committee member told the Eighth Party Congress.[258] The power of the bureaucracy, and within the bureaucracy the power of its top layers, grew.

The Bolshevik Party itself had undergone dramatic changes. By the end of the civil war only one party member in every ten actually worked in a factory,[259] six out of every ten were employed in the government or party machine and a quarter of party members served in the Red Army, often in positions of political or military authority. The military often returned home and 'assumed leading posts in the local soviets, in the economy, in education and they persistently introduced everywhere that regime which ensured success in the civil war', argued Trotsky in *The Revolution Betrayed*.[260]

The need for discipline during the civil war, for centralisation, was not something simply foisted on the party by the leadership. It was a pressing need felt by the rank and file members every bit as much as by the leadership:

> There were times between 1918 and 1921, indeed, when Lenin and his associates lagged somewhat behind a vociferous body of local opinion which urged an extension and reinforcement of the centralising and disciplinary trends...[261]
>
> ...[I]t was the civil war which did the trick. Almost overnight it was witnessed that nearly all those dyed-in-the-wool defenders of local rights in 1917 were now ready, however reluctantly, to recognise that the military crisis called for the introduction of stern internal discipline.[262]

The Tenth Party Congress was a traumatic experience. The crisis of War Communism produced a massive wave of debate and opposition among the Bolsheviks. There were no fewer than eight different platforms put forward by different groups and individuals. The Workers' Opposition presented an extensive critique of the direction the regime was heading. The Workers' Opposition wanted to reform the system by handing power to the trade unions and workers in the factories. The difficulty was that the working class, as we have seen, had been decimated. The Workers' Opposition's plans could only have led to a disintegration of the regime.

Lenin had a different two fold solution. Firstly, he wanted to stop the party—which he described as 'sick, feverish'—from tearing itself apart under the pressure of events. He declared:

> There should not be the slightest trace of factionalism—whatever its manifestations in the past. That we must not have on any account [when there is a] tremendous preponderance of peasants in the country, when their dissatisfaction with the proletarian dictatorship is mounting, and when the demobilisation of the peasant army is setting loose hundreds and thousands of broken men

who have nothing to do, whose only accustomed occupation is war and who breed banditry. The atmosphere of the controversy is becoming extremely dangerous and constitutes a direct threat to the dictatorship of the proletariat.[263]

The Congress voted to ban factions. Again it was not simply a leadership diktat. Radek spoke for many when he told the Congress:

> In voting for this resolution, I feel that it can well be turned against us, nevertheless I support it. Let the Central Committee in a moment of danger take the severest measures against the best party comrades, if it finds this necessary. Let the Central Committee even be mistaken! That is less dangerous than the wavering which is now observable.[264]

Neither was the ban considered total or permanent. When one senior Bolshevik tried to get the Congress to agree a ban on separate platforms in Central Committee elections, Lenin replied:

> We cannot deprive the party and the members of the Central Committee of the right to appeal to the party in the event of disagreement on fundamental issues. Supposing we are faced with a question like, say, the conclusion of the Brest peace? Can you guarantee that no such question will arise? No, you cannot. In the circumstances, the elections may have to be based on platforms.[265]

Secondly, Lenin fought, in the last battle of his life, to reform the bureaucracy from within. He said:

> You can throw out the Tsar, throw out the landowners, throw out the capitalists but you cannot 'throw out' the bureaucracy in a peasant country... You can only *reduce* it by slow and stubborn effort...for many years to come.[266]

Lenin sought Trotsky's aid in undermining Stalin's growing power, he fought to strengthen the Workers' and Peasants' Inspectorate which was meant to counter bureaucratic abuse and he tried to combat the growing Russian chauvinism in the state machine. But Lenin's worsening health hampered him. He first became ill in mid-1921, suffered a stroke in May 1922, returned to work but fell ill again in December 1922. In March 1923 he was again stricken by a stroke which left him partially paralysed and virtually unable to speak until his death in January 1924. His last notes were insistent that Stalin should be removed from the post of General Secretary.

But Lenin's last battle, like Trotsky's opposition to Stalin which began in 1923, suffered from a fundamental weakness. After the war the regime was left stranded. The well head of renewal and thorough reform—the activity of the workers—had dried to a trickle. Bureaucratic abuse and corruption were the inevitable result. To appeal outside the machine, as the Workers' Opposition had wanted, was impossible. This is the tragedy of Lenin's last fight and of the Left Opposition. They knew the problem but the means at their disposal was not equal to the task. Hence the paucity of the measures they advocated: self reform of the bureaucracy. Here is the root of Trotsky's defeat. To fight within the bureaucracy was to fight on terms more favourable to Stalin than to Trotsky. Trotsky's strength, like Lenin's, had always been his link with the workers. From them he drew inspiration. On them he placed all his hopes for a socialist society. Against their experience he judged the correctness of his strategy. And, most of all, it was on the consciousness and organisation of the workers that he relied in every major struggle.

Stalin, by contrast, relied on the machine—on the committee, the threat, the order and the bribe. He was determined to 'bury Trotskyism', insisting that the Trotskyist 'cadres can be removed only by civil war'. And civil war there was. It began with Opposition speakers being heckled and assaulted. Then the whole vast propaganda machine of the bureaucracy was turned against them. Later, they were exiled, imprisoned and shot.

The Trotskyist Opposition fought courageously. It sometimes saw its arguments gaining considerable ground among party members. Many party members, especially the experienced party members who had lived and fought through 1917, were supporters of the Opposition.

But ultimately, without a revival of struggle in Russia or successful revolution elsewhere, the Opposition was doomed to failure. That, however, could not be known in advance. Trotsky fought on, even though the ground on which he stood was being consumed by fire, in the hope that a revival of domestic or international struggle would come to his aid. The only other choice was capitulation.

The Trotskyists' struggle delayed Stalin's rise to power, a rise which was only complete after the Left Opposition was broken in 1928, not before. This is why the majority of historians note the difference between the 'revolution' from above which came after 1928 and the period before 1928. The struggle of the Left Opposition also made it obvious that Stalin was the betrayer of the revolution and that his regime was the counter-revolutionary antithesis of the October revolution. Stalin's regime not only reversed every remaining gain of October but had to annihilate the entire leadership and many of the ordinary Bolsheviks who had made the October revolution. The fact that he could do so by administrative terror, not by the more normal means of an armed counter-revolutionary seizure of power, was a result of the atom-isation of the working class. No wider use of force was necessary, no martial law, no curfew or street battles, because the condition of the working class had reduced the battle between revolution and counter-revolution to a struggle concerning, albeit not exclu-sively, different sections of the Bolshevik party. This should not blind us to the scale of the counter-revolution which did take place, to the essential difference between the Stalin regime and even the regime of the mid-1920s. Stephen Cohen argues:

> Stalin's new policies of 1929-33, the 'great change' as they became known, were a radical departure from Bolshevik programmatic thinking. No Bolshevik leader or faction had ever advocated any-thing akin to imposed collectivisation, the 'liquidation' of allegedly prosperous peasants (kulaks), breakneck heavy industrialisation, the destruction of the entire market sector, and a 'plan' that was in reality no plan at all, only hyper-centralised control of the econ-omy plus exhortations. These years of 'revolution from above' were, historically and programmatically, the birth period of Stalinism.[267]

Michael Reiman's invaluable *The Birth of Stalinism* arrives at similar conclusions by tracing in impressive detail the complete-ness of this rupture.[268] Cohen also argues:

> Official ideology changed radically under Stalin. Several of those changes have been noted by Western and Soviet scholars: the revival of nationalism, statism, anti-Semitism, and conservative, or reactionary, cultural and behavioural norms; the repeal of ideas and legislation favouring workers, women, schoolchildren, minor-ity cultures, and egalitarianism, as well as a host of revolutionary and Bolshevik symbols; and a switch in emphasis from ordinary people to leaders and official bosses as the creators of history.

They were not simply amendments but a new ideology that was 'changed in *essence*' and that did 'not represent the same movement as that which took power in 1917'.[269]

The point is not to idealise the Bolshevik regime of the early 1920s. Of course they had arrived at a point far distant from the goals of 1917. This analysis is merely meant to demonstrate two points. Firstly, it was overwhelmingly the force of circumstance which obliged the Bolsheviks to retreat so far from their goals. They travelled this route in opposition to their own theory, not because of it—no matter what rhetorical justifications were given at the time. And secondly, the alternatives available at the time were worse than the Bolsheviks. Even those movements which, on paper, appeared to have a more democratic programme (Workers' Opposition, Kronstadt, Makhno) were either frauds (Makhno) or utopians. They were utopians because they looked back to the institutions of 1917 when the class which made such institutions possible no longer had the collective capability to direct political life. This is the tragedy of the early 1920s: the Bolsheviks had beaten their opponents by destroying the base on which they stood—literally destroyed it by death incurred at the front or by depopulating the cities as a result of starvation, disease and flight to the country. The lack of democracy was a result of this, not a first cause. The secret of the Stalinist bureaucracy's success lay in the devastation and isolation of the workers' state.

The October revolution and politics today

In many major industrialised countries the 1980s were mostly a period of retreat for the workers' movement and the left, irrespective of whether right wing governments (Reagan, Thatcher, Kohl) or right wing social democratic governments (Mitterrand, Hawke, Gonzales) were in power. Under these conditions very considerable sections of the left began to evolve, first, in the direction of left reformism. This was the era of infatuation with the Labour left in Britain, the Socialist Party in France, PASOK in Greece, the collapse of the Italian revolutionary left and the rise of movementism internationally. Latterly, faced with the failure of these projects and very much under the influence of events in Eastern Europe and the consequent collapse of the Western

83

Communist Parties, this evolution tended toward outright and almost unqualified identification with bourgeois democracy, at least in intellectual circles.

This process was accelerated by the second Gulf War, during which a number of socialists (Norman Geras and Fred Halliday in Britain, for instance) decided to back US and British imperialism. Significant numbers of others, notably the editorial board of *New Left Review*, were, at best, careful to couch their partial opposition in terms circumscribed by bourgeois democracy (support for sanctions, advocacy of the UN). The result is that much of what now passes for socialist thought is indistinguishable from run of the mill liberalism. The swelling literature on citizenship, democratic and constitutional reform, the virtues of civil society and so on are the unmistakable symbols of this process. In this world the superiority of the market is taken as axiomatic.

In these developments the history of the October revolution has a key place. Once the argument that Lenin led to Stalin is established, any alternative to the market and bourgeois democracy becomes that much more difficult to make. To stray from the straight and narrow road walked by J S Mill and Adam Smith is to court the gulag. We live in the best of all possible worlds, runs the argument, and the fate of the October revolution demonstrates the foolhardiness of trying to change it. Paul Hirst, now a leading figure in the civil rights group Charter 88, has latterly become so convinced that the market and the rule of law are the only viable forms of society that any vision of an alternative— whether Lenin's or the eco-social democracy of Vaclav Havel—are treated as dangerous utopian dreams.[270]

Robin Blackburn's attempt to try and find the non-existent thread that is supposed to connect those high priests of the free market, von Mises and von Hayek, with Trotsky is another response to these developments. Blackburn's point seems to be that, as Trotsky argued that some form of market mechanism would be used in the transition to a communist society, the leader of the Russian Revolution must have something in common with today's descendants of von Hayek and von Mises. The small question of which class is in power, the capitalist class or the working class, does not impinge on this analysis. Or at least it only impinges to the extent that the market is assumed to be a strategy for gaining power, rather than a mechanism that may be used, under greatly altered conditions, once a revolution has succeeded.

It is, then, merely the difference between reform and revolution.

So many of these arguments depend on a revival, in whole or in part, of an essentially Cold War interpretation of the Russian Revolution. Yet if the history of the October revolution is not as one time socialists would have us believe, then the workers' movement of today still has a powerful weapon in its armoury. Mass unemployment, war and imperialism, third world starvation and first world poverty, homelessness and economic exploitation, racism and sexism, anti-union laws and, at best, castrated political rights are not all that the world has to offer. Then the unprecedented political freedom, the cultural and artistic explosion, the unique economic liberation, the sexual and national risings that were the hallmark of the early days of the October revolution, and which this essay on the dark hours of the revolution has had little time to consider, are still within our reach. The October revolution is our past. It is also our future. We should not relinquish it so easily.

My thanks to the following for their comments on the first draft: Tony Cliff, Nikolai Genchev, Lindsey German, Chris Harman, Mike Haynes, John Molyneux, Pete Morgan and, especially, to Nikolai Preobrazhensky.

1 W Rees-Mogg, *Independent*, 14 October 1989. R Pipes, *The Russian Revolution* (London, 1990).
2 *Moscow News*, weekly, No 2, 1991.
3 See Jonathan Steele, 'Solzhenitsyn Off The Press, Trotsky Under Wraps', *Guardian*, 6 May 1991.
4 Private communication from a Moscow based socialist.
5 See 'A Shade Less Red', *Daily Mail*, 8 February 1990.
6 'Waking From History's Great Dream', *Independent on Sunday*, 4 February 1990.
7 See J Slovo, 'Socialist Aspirations and Socialist Realities', *The African Communist*, No 124, (Johannesburg, 1991), p9. Similar but more coded formulations appear in J Slovo, *Has Socialism Failed?* (London, 1990).
8 R Blackburn, 'Fin de Siècle: Socialism after the Crash', *New Left Review* 185, January/February 1991, p21.
9 P Hirst, 'The State, Civil Society and the Collapse of Soviet Communism', *Economy and Society*, Volume 20, No.2, May 1991, p219.
10 S Farber, *Before Stalinism* (Polity Press, 1991), pp99 and 109.
11 See *Against the Current*, Nos 29 and 32 (Detroit). The particularly right wing, anti-Leninist account is T Shanin, 'The Ethics of Socialist Praxis', *Against the Current*, No 32, pp43-5.
12 See S Farber, op cit, p12.
13 B Kagarlitsky, *The Thinking Reed* (London, 1988), pp41 and 65, although the general tenor of Kagarlitsky's account is less critical of the Bolsheviks in this work than in his later *The Dialectic of Change*. Possibly this is because *The Thinking Reed* was written when the opposition movement barely existed and when the decay of the regime was not so advanced.

14 R Blackburn, op cit, p8.
15 L Trotsky, 'Results and Prospects' in *The Permanent Revolution and Results and Prospects* (New York, 1969), p105.
16 Quoted in E H Carr, *The Bolshevik Revolution 1917-1923*, Vol III (London, 1966), p9.
17 Ibid, pp17-18.
18 Ibid, p53.
19 R Blackburn, op cit, p24.
20 E H Carr, op cit, p59.
21 Quoted in L Trotsky, op cit, p105.
22 K Kautsky, *The Dictatorship of the Proletariat* (University of Michigan, 1964), p64.
23 V Serge, *Year One Of the Russian Revolution* (London, 1972), pp314-315.
24 V Serge, *Destiny of a Revolution* (London, 1937), p144.
25 V Serge, *Year One...*, op cit, p325.
26 Quoted in T Cliff, *Lenin*, Vol 4: *The Bolsheviks and the World Revolution* (London, 1979), p8.
27 See T Cliff, *Trotsky*, Vol 2, 1917-1923, *The Sword of the Revolution* (Bookmarks, 1990), p211.
28 Marx, *Selected Correspondence* (Moscow, 1956), p320.
29 See 'The Berlin USPD debate on the National Assembly' in *The Third International in Lenin's Time, The German Revolution and the Debate on Soviet Power, documents: 1918-1919* (New York, 1986), p128.
30 E Acton, *Rethinking the Russian Revolution* (London, 1990), p2.
31 R Pipes, op cit, p491.
32 Quoted in W Bruce Lincoln, *Red Victory* (New York, 1989), pp28, 39-40.
33 Quoted in M Ferro, *October 1917, a Social History of the Russian Revolution* (London, 1980), p14.
34 L Trotsky, *History of the Russian Revolution* (London, 1977), p240.
35 Quoted in R Medvedev, *The October Revolution* (New York, 1979), p69.
36 V Serge, *Year One...*, op cit, p109.
37 M Jones, 'Year of Two Revolutions', in M Jones (ed), *Storming the Heavens, Voices of October* (London, 1987), pxliii.
38 Quoted in ibid, pxlv.
39 W Bruce Lincoln, op cit, p35.
40 The Bolsheviks withdrew the slogan, 'All power to the soviets', after the defeat of the July Days since they worried that the leadership of the soviets had irretrievably fallen into the hands of the moderate socialists. Instead they briefly based their strategy on the more responsive local factory committees. When the popular mood turned decisively against the Provisional Government and the moderates in the soviets the Bolsheviks returned to their original formulation. None of this alters the essence of the Bolsheviks' strategy which was to take power from the Provisional Government and put it in the hands of popular organs of working class power—a point later made explicit by Trotsky in his *The Lessons of October* (Bookmarks, 1987).
41 M Jones, op cit, pxlv.
42 Ibid.
43 M Ferro, op cit, p37.
44 L Trotsky, *History...*, op cit, p668.
45 See M Ferro, op cit, p51.
46 Ibid, p46.
47 Quoted in R Medvedev, op cit, pp70-1.
48 N Podvoisky, 'Lenin—Organiser of the Victorious October Uprising', in

M Jones (ed), *Storming the Heavens...*, op cit, p116.

49 Lenin, *Collected Works*, Vol 26, p212. For 'Marxism and Insurrection', see *Collected Works*, Vol 26, pp22-7. Also see N Harding, *Lenin's Political Thought*, Vol 2, *Theory and Practice in the Socialist Revolution* (London, 1983), p164.

50 N N Sukhanov, *The Russian Revolution 1917, a Personal Record* (Princeton University Press, 1984), p576.

51 R Service, *The Bolshevik Party in Revolution: a Study in Organisational Change 1917-23* (London, 1979), p62.

52 Quoted in T Cliff, *Lenin*, Vol 3, *The Revolution Besieged*, (London, 1978), p2.

53 S Cohen, *Rethinking the Soviet Experience* (Oxford, 1985), p5. Probably the best known of the Cold War historians is Leonard Shapiro. Cohen provides an impressive list of quotes about the 'straight line' from Lenin to Stalin on pp42-43.

54 S Farber, op cit, pp149-150.

55 R Blackburn, op cit, pp20-2.

56 See Lenin, *Collected Works*, Vol 8, p117. See also p141: 'Social democracy...was still weak, weak in comparison with the overwhelming demand of the active proletarian masses for social democratic leadership.'

57 R Service, op cit, p36.

58 Ibid, p58.

59 Ibid, p84.

60 Ibid, pp210-11.

61 Ibid, p52.

62 Ibid, p3.

63 Quoted in ibid, p61.

64 For a full treatment of these issues see C Harman, *The Lost Revolution, Germany 1918 to 1923* (Bookmarks, 1997), particularly chapter 5.

65 R Blackburn, op cit, p23.

66 Ibid, p10.

67 T Wohlforth, 'Transition to the Transition', *New Left Review* 130, November/December 1981, p79.

68 S Farber, op cit, p56.

69 R Luxemburg, 'The Russian Revolution', in Mary-Alice Waters (ed), *Rosa Luxemburg Speaks* (New York, 1970), p375.

70 Quoted in R Medvedev, op cit, pp103-104.

71 Ibid, p108.

72 V Serge, *Year One...*, p130.

73 Quoted in M Liebman, *Leninism Under Lenin* (London, 1975), p245.

74 R Medvedev, op cit, pp110-11. Since the elections were conducted on the basis of proportional representation the LSR results are even more impressive than they seem at first sight.

75 See R Medvedev, op cit, pp110-12.

76 Figures from Lenin, 'The Proletarian Revolution and -the Renegade Kautsky', in *The Third International in Lenin's Time...*, op cit, p357.

77 V Serge, *Year One...*, op cit, p131.

78 Ibid, pp130-31.

79 L Shapiro, *1917: The Russian Revolutions and the Origins of Present-Day Communism* (London, 1984), p149.

80 W H Chamberlin, *The Russian Revolution*, Vol I, 1917-1918, from the overthrow of the Tsar to the assumption of power by the Bolsheviks (Princeton University Press, 1987), p370. W H Chamberlin's history is important since his account is based on material available to him during

his stay in Moscow (1922-1934), but unavailable to many historians during the Stalin and Cold War periods. R Pipes, op cit, p555, lacks any such qualification.

81 See, for instance, K Kautsky, 'National Assembly and Council Assembly', in *The Third International in Lenin's Time...*, op cit, pp94-105.

82 Ibid, p138.

83 Ibid, p94.

84 M Liebman, op cit, p236.

85 Quoted in V Serge, *Year One...*, op cit, pp342-43.

86 J Slovo, 'Socialist Aspirations...', op cit, p9. This is the literary equivalent of the tactic now being pursued by museum curators in Moscow: Trotsky's portrait has been restored to the galleries, but it is always placed alongside Stalin's. The meaning is unspoken but clear: 'Stalin was bad, but so was Trotsky so there is no point in looking to him for an alternative.' Slovo makes the point explicit: 'I believe we should exercise some caution before we accept Pallo Jordan's rather sweeping judgement that we must turn to the works of "oppositionists" (including Trotsky), to discover the true meaning of the communist vision.'

87 R Blackburn, op cit, p21.

88 S Farber, op cit, p44.

89 J Slovo, op cit, p8.

90 S Farber, op cit, p47.

91 Ibid, p117.

92 V Serge, *Year One...*, op cit, p350.

93 T Cliff, *Lenin*, Vol 3 (London. 1978), p68.

94 V Serge, *Year One...*, op cit, pp350-352.

95 W Bruce Lincoln, op cit, p50.

96 Quoted in W H Chamberlin, *The Russian Revolution*, Vol II,1918-1921 (Princeton University Press, 1987), p78.

97 Ibid, p59.

98 W H Chamberlin, Vol I, op cit, p371.

99 R Pipes, op cit, p790.

100 V Serge, *Year One...*, op cit, pp187-88.

101 Ibid, p189.

102 A F Upton, *The Finnish Revolution, 1917-1918* (University of Minnesota Press, 1980), p519.

103 Ibid, p521.

104 Ibid.

105 Ibid.

106 Ibid, p522.

107 Ibid, pp89-90.

108 V Serge, *Year One...*, op cit, p349.

109 W Bruce Lincoln, op cit, p99.

110 Ibid, p198.

111 L Trotsky, *My Life* (New York, 1960), pp396–97.

112 Quoted in W Bruce Lincoln, op cit, p204.

113 Ibid, p225.

114 Ibid, p226.

115 Ibid, pp88-9.

116 Ibid, p100.

117 V Serge, *Year One...*, op cit, p333.

118 Quoted in W Bruce Lincoln, op cit, p86.

119 W Bruce Lincoln, op cit, pp48-9.

120 Ibid, p321.

121 Ibid, p317.

122 Ibid, pp322-3.
123 Ibid.
124 Ibid, pp319-20. It is worth noting that, even if the most exaggerated claims for the killings of the Cheka were true, 140,000 over the whole of the civil war (see Pipes, op cit, p838), this figure is still lower than the number of Jews murdered by the Whites in just one area, in just one year: the Ukraine in 1919.
125 Quoted ibid, p259.
126 Ibid, p256.
127 See ibid, pp256-57.
128 Quoted ibid, p259.
129 R Lucken, The White Generals (London, 1971), p184.
130 W Bruce Lincoln, op cit, p210.
131 R Luckett, op cit, p255.
132 Quoted in W Bruce Lincoln, op cit, pp436-37.
133 Quoted in W H Chamberlin, op cit, Vol II, (Princeton University Press, 1987), p197.
134 Quoted in W Bruce Lincoln, op cit, p247 and p263.
135 Quoted ibid, p263.
136 Quoted in W H Chamberlin, Vol II, op cit, p403.
137 Quoted in W Bruce Lincoln, op cit, p283.
138 W H Chamberlin, Vol II, op cit, p138.
139 Quoted in ibid, p261.
140 Ibid, p283.
141 Ibid, p169.
142 W Bruce Lincoln, op cit, p294.
143 W H Chamberlin, Vol II, op cit, p258.
144 See W Bruce Lincoln, op cit, pp280-82.
145 W H Chamberlin, Vol II, op cit, p461.
146 W Bruce Lincoln, op cit, p266.
147 T Cliff, 'Trotsky on Substitutionism', International Socialism (first series), No 2, Autumn 1960.
148 S A Smith, Red Petrograd (Cambridge University Press, 1983), p210. Indeed one of Lenin's first articles on the economy after the revolution was entitled 'How to organise competition?' and insisted: 'Now that a socialist government is in power our task is to organise competition.' Collected Works, Vol 26, p404.
149 S A Smith, ibid, p209.
150 Ibid, pp220-21.
151 Ibid, pp222-23.
152 See T Cliff, Lenin Vol 3, op cit, p81.
153 Ibid, p81. S A Smith, op cit, also charts this process in some detail, see, for instance, pp238-39. He also points out that some workers' takeovers were meant to push the government into taking some share in management because 'workers' management proved incapable of dealing with the immense problems affecting production', especially in the big factories.
154 Kritzman quoted in T Cliff, Lenin Vol 3, op cit, p83.
155 See W Bruce Lincoln, op cit, p116.
156 Ibid, pp115-16.
157 Quoted in S A Smith, op cit, p239.
158 V Serge, Year One..., op cit, p353.
159 S A Smith, op cit, p242.
160 S A Smith, op cit, pp250-51.
161 Quoted in L T Lih, 'Bolshevik, Razvertsha and War Communism', Slavic

Review Vol 48, No. 4, 1986, p679.

162 P Avrich, *Kronstadt 1921* (Princeton University Press, 1991), p19.

163 Cited in W Bruce Lincoln, op cit, p63.

164 See S Farber, op cit, p70.

165 Quoted in L T Lih, op cit, p678-79.

166 W Bruce Lincoln, op cit, p65.

167 Ibid, p480 and p416.

168 Quoted ibid, p345.

169 W H Chamberlin, Vol II, op cit, p347.

170 W H Chamberlin, Vol I, op cit, p332, and Vol II, pp68-9.

171 P Knightley, *The Second Oldest Profession* (London, 1986), pp57-72.

172 Ibid, pp57-8.

173 Quoted in T Cliff, *Lenin* Vol 4, op cit, p18.

174 See T Cliff, *Trotsky*, Vol 2, op cit, pp32-3.

175 G Leggett, *The Cheka: Lenin's Political Police* (Oxford, 1981), p21.

176 Ibid, pp30, 35-7.

177 W Bruce Lincoln, op cit, p138.

178 Ibid, p127.

179 Quoted in Knightley, op cit, p75.

180 See, for instance, W H Chamberlin Vol II, op cit, pp70-1.

181 G Leggett, op cit, pp130-31.

182 Ibid, p197. Leggett also cites S P Melgounov's *The Red Terror in Russia*. But Leggett is quite wrong to describe Melgounov as a 'respected socialist politician' (p185). Melgounov's account is partial and filled with unbalanced judgements. For instance, 'Not for nothing do the three letters which stand for the title of the All-Russian Extraordinary Commission of the Cheka stand also for the three Russian words which denote "Death to every man".' (!), p41.

183 G Leggett, op cit, pp168-69.

184 See G Leggett, op cit, pp176-82.

185 For instance the Cheka executed prisoners the night before the death penalty was abolished in 1920. See Mary McAuley, *Bread and Authority: State and Society in Petrograd 1917-1922* (Oxford, 1991), p391. The Cheka also carried out executions by transferring prisoners to front line areas when the death penalty was abolished in the rear during the civil war. Further evidence that, unlike the White Terror, the Red Terror was more severe the further it was from the leadership is contained in McAuley, p386: 'As in the French revolution...terror was worse in provincial towns...than in capital cities. It was the terrible provincial blood letting that caused the concern in the party press of October-December 1918...the terror of September and October provoked a reaction within the party and was tacitly abandoned within a few weeks.'

186 R Pipes, op cit, p792.

187 V Serge, *Year One...*, op cit, pp326–27.

188 Quoted in R Medvedev, *Let History Judge* (Oxford, 1989), p502.

189 Ibid.

190 See B Kagarlitsky, op cit, p53.

191 Quoted in R Medvedev, *Let History Judge,* op cit, p655.

192 Ibid, p654.

193 Lenin, *Collected Works* Vol 28, p389.

194 G Leggett, op cit, p187.

195 Quoted in W Bruce Lincoln, op cit, p139.

196 Quoted in G Leggett. op cit, p162.

197 Ibid, p161.

198 Ibid, p171.

199 Quoted ibid, p357.
200 Ibid, p188.
201 Quoted ibid, p189.
202 Ibid, p342.
203 Quoted ibid.
204 Ibid, p345.
205 R Medvedev, *Let History Judge,* op cit, p656.
206 Ibid, p657
207 Quoted in G Leggett, op cit, p163.
208 Quoted in W Bruce Lincoln, op cit, p364.
209 Ibid, p371.
210 Ibid, p364.
211 Ibid, pp372-73.
212 See T Cliff, *Lenin* Vol 3, op cit, p95.
213 Quoted in W Bruce Lincoln, op cit, p358.
214 W H Chamberlin, Vol II, op cit, p432.
215 S Farber, op cit, pp122-124.
216 W Bruce Lincoln, op cit, pp468-70.
217 Ibid, p471.
218 Ibid.
219 M Palij, *The Anarchism of Nestor Makhno* (University of Washington Press, 1976), p177.
220 W H Chamberlin, Vol II, op cit, p237.
221 Ibid, pp237-238.
222 See W Bruce Lincoln, op cit, p327.
223 M Palij, op cit, p219.
224 Ibid, p214.
225 P Avrich, *Anarchist Portraits* (Princeton University Press, 1988), pp120-121.
226 Ibid, p120.
227 M Armstrong, 'Nestor Makhno: the failure of anarchism' in *Socialist Review* (Australia), Summer 1990, No 3, p114.
228 M Palij, op cit, p214.
229 Ibid, pp213-14.
230 P Avrich, *Anarchist...*, op cit, pl 14.
231 W H Chamberlin, Vol II, op cit, p236.
232 P Avrich, *Anarchist...*, op cit, p121.
233 See M Palij, op cit, p152.
234 W H Chamberlin, Vol II, pp234 and 232.
235 See F Sysyn, 'Nestor Makhno and the Ukrainian Revolution', in T Hunczak (ed), *The Ukraine 1917-1921 a Study in Revolution* (Harvard University Press, 1977), p290 n49. Makhno seems to have had two 'wives'. The one who headed the Punitive Commission is not the one who kept the diary quoted earlier in the text.
236 D Footman, *Civil War in Russia* (London, 1961), p288.
237 Ibid, p282.
238 I Getzler, *Kronstadt 1917-1921* (London, 1983), pp206-07.
239 See D Fedotoff White, *The Growth of the Red Army* (Princeton University Press, 1944), p154.
240 Ibid, p140.
241 Ibid, p142.
242 Ibid, p143.
243 S Farber, op cit, pp192-93.
244 Quoted in W Bruce Lincoln, op cit, p495.
245 P Avrich, *Kronstadt...*, op cit, pp94-5.

246 Quoted in I Getzler, op cit, pp209-10.
247 P Avrich, *Kronstadt...*, op cit, p68.
248 Ibid, pp63-6.
249 'What We Are Fighting For' in P Avrich, ibid, pp242-43.
250 See P Avrich, *Kronstadt...*, op cit, p240.
251 Ibid, pp 107, 121-22.
252 Ibid, pp110-11.
253 Ibid, pp127-28.
254 Quoted in T Cliff, *Lenin* Vol 4, op cit, p134.
255 Quoted in P Avrich, *Kronstadt...*, opcit, p222.
256 Quoted in T Cliff, *Trotsky* Vol 2, op cit, p188.
257 Quoted ibid, p193.
258 Quoted in W Bruce Lincoln, op cit, p479.
259 Indeed the situation was even worse than this: of those who worked in factories most were in administration, not 'at the bench'.
260 Quoted in M von Hagen, *Soldiers in the Proletarian Dictatorship* (Cornell University Press, 1990), p5.
261 R Service, op cit, p8.
262 Ibid, p208.
263 Quoted in T Cliff, *Lenin* Vol 4, op cit, p136.
264 Ibid, p138.
265 Ibid, p137.
266 Quoted in W Bruce Lincoln, op cit, p380.
267 S Cohen, op cit, p62.
268 M Reiman, *The Birth of Stalinism* (London, 1987).
269 S Cohen, op cit, p52.
270 P Hirst, op cit, pp224-25.

2

Did Lenin lead to Stalin?

Robert Service

Very few scholars and commentators nowadays contend that there was an inevitability about the passage from the political, economic and social policies of Lenin to the Stalinist programme of the 1930s and 1940s. Stalin introduced a régime of long term mass terror. Stalin imposed a grotesque and uniform official ideology, ludicrously overstating his own merits—even at the expense of Lenin. He completely rewrote history. Stalin had dictatorial power over his party, his government and the state. He exercised this power with systematic and extreme brutality over a period of more than 20 years. Stalin also brought into direct or semi-direct state ownership every single sector of the economy: trade, agriculture, industry and banking. And Stalin initiated a covert policy of Russian nationalism, spilling over into virulent anti-Semitism in the post-war years: the Bolshevik leader from Georgia was the greatest Russian chauvinist of them all.

Undeniably Lenin did much to distance himself from Stalin. In 1922-3, as he lay on his deathbed and composed his political testament, he recommended Stalin's removal from the General Secretaryship of the Russian Communist Party's Central Committee. There can be no clearer indication of the alienation of the founder of the Soviet state from the colleague who directed the party's administrative machinery. No other Politburo member had earned so fierce a criticism from Lenin.

Even so, Lenin by no means suggested that Stalin should be ejected entirely from the party leadership; and he certainly did not propose the expulsion of Joseph Stalin from the party: in the 1920s such a suggestion would have been inconceivable. Stalin's sins were many in Lenin's judgement. Yet these did not induce him to seek to terminate his political career. Nor did Lenin, even on his deathbed, rehearse some of the nastier elements of Stalin's past—elements that were visible even in the civil war. When Stalin was on the southern front in mid-1918, for example, he had encouraged a mass terror and a fundamental lawlessness that was notorious in the Tsaritsyn region. Lenin had not disciplined him over that nor did he see fit to include any reproof in his political testament.

Lenin also had an especially bossy personality. Once he had taken against someone in a particular matter, he tended to get pre-occupied and even obsessed. His illness aggravated this trait. His spat with Stalin in 1922-3 over foreign trade, bureaucracy and the federal constitution made him beside himself with fury against one of the two Bolshevik leaders whom he identified as his likely successors. A psychological factor was involved: and only those who like their politics to consist of the purest saints and entirely irredeemable villains find this an uncomfortable observation.

Consequently, although much attention is paid to what divided Lenin and Stalin in those crucial years, we must not overlook what continued to unite them. The unifying points go unmentioned in the testament for the precise reason that they were not divisive. Among them were the belief of both of them in dictatorship; in the one party state; in the continued deployment of terror whenever the party's power was thought to be threatened; in the imposition of a single unchallengeable ideology; in the subjugation of all public institutions and mass organisations to the will of the party; in the strictest internal party discipline; in the efficacy of crude political language and methods; in the need to indoctrinate the working class.

This system of beliefs was in a condition of partial construction before the October revolution. The scaffolding for its walls was in place by the middle of the civil war. The roof was added at the inception of the New Economic Policy in 1921. The collective architect was the central and local party leadership, and its major thinker and planner was Vladimir Lenin.

And what about this Lenin? There is natural sympathy for him in 1922-4. The effort needed to dictate his last thoughts to a group of secretaries was enormous. After his physical collapse in spring 1922, he had only residual use of his limbs and his power of speech was limited; and he was kept isolated in the government sanatorium at Gorki, tended by several Russian and German doctors and by his wife Nadezhda and sister Maria. He was dying, and knew it. He was only in his early fifties. Had disease not struck him down, there was every reason to expect that he would continue to guide the Bolshevik Party and Soviet state. What became known as his political testament were words extricated from a still lucid mind by a man determined that he would not leave this life before communicating his worries to party comrades.

No wonder that Gorbachev encouraged professional Soviet historians to accentuate the importance of this last period in Lenin's life. Here was Lenin apparently at his gentlest. Lenin the harrier of Stalin and his cronies. Lenin of the New Economic Policy. Lenin the protector of the peasants. Lenin the advocate of commercial interests and of concessions to private enterprise. Lenin the opponent of bureaucrats and nationalists. Nor was this an image of Lenin which was confined to the Soviet Union. On the contrary, Lenin as the embodiment of Soviet communism with a human face has been a widely, albeit not universally, reproduced picture in the West.

The portrait bears as little relation to reality as Holbein's representation of Anne of Cleves for the delectation of Henry VIII. Lenin, after introducing the New Economic Policy in 1921, by no means rejected terror. Admittedly he narrowed the range of its operations. But certain social categories could expect no mercy. For example, it was in 1922 that he recommended the arrest and execution of Russian Orthodox Church bishops. This was said in the privacy of Politburo discussions. His plan derived not from the revelation of some definite anti-regime plot but rather from a wish to terrorise the clergy into a condition of fear which would last decades.

Cultural controls were tightened under the New Economic Policy. To be sure, there remained much latitude for creative self expression. The murderously bizarre attempts at monolithism in the 1930s were as yet unimagined. But the New Economic Policy, coming after an exhausting civil war, was used by Lenin

95

to assert the party's general authority in areas of social life previously touched little by him. Thus Lenin was responsible for the expulsion from Soviet Russia of dozens of leading philosophers, poets and novelists in 1922. Lenin in the last phase of his career was far from being a 'liberal' communist in policy for the arts.

Least of all was he liberal towards outright political adversaries. He refused to revoke the ban on internal factions he had imposed at the Tenth Party Congress in March 1921. Nothing in his testament indicated a change of mind. Expulsion from the party was his ambition for Alexander Shlyapnikov's Workers' Opposition if the Opposition refused to cease activity. This, however, was mild in comparison with his attitude to non-Bolshevik political opponents. In 1922 he notoriously demanded that the leadership of the Party of Socialist Revolutionaries be arrested, put on trial and executed. Negotiations about the Civil Code in the same year, moreover, demonstrated a readiness to treat the Mensheviks with the same ruthlessness. Only the intervention of his central party colleagues stopped him from acting quite so dictatorially towards rival parties.

But what about Lenin's economic policy in 1921? Certainly he aimed at short term concessions to private enterprise after the civil war. But his projections in the medium term were for increased state intervention, increased state regulation, increased state ownership. The New Economic Policy was only a strategic manoeuvre. Furthermore, Lenin had no realistic answer to the aggravation of bureaucratic problems that any future amassment of state-economic authority would involve.

Nor did Lenin have much practical respect for national self determination. A dispute occurred between him and Stalin over proposals for a federal constitution in 1922. The specific bone of contention was Stalin's wish to deprive his native Georgia of its republican status and push it into a Transcaucasian republic which would seek incorporation in the greater Soviet Union. Lenin, on reflection, demurred but found Stalin reluctant to give way to him. And yet not even in the heat of the controversy did Lenin differ from Stalin in wishing to deny national self determination to the Georgian people. Both took it for granted that the Georgians would be held in the USSR willy nilly. No plebiscite would be held. And the central party leaders in Moscow would ensure Georgian political compliance by maintaining direct control over the Georgian communist party. Georgia's subjection to the

Kremlin would be sternly enforced.

Lenin's last struggle, then, was certainly the struggle of a dying man who fought right to the end and passed away with dignity. But Lenin also died a Bolshevik; and his Bolshevism contained many genes which were to produce Stalinism in the following decade.

If Lenin had been a fit man and had lived into that decade, the theories and policies and practices of his party would have been different from Stalin's in several basic respects. It over-stretches belief that Lenin would have exterminated his close colleagues or that he would deliberately have sent millions to their deaths in the blood purges of the late 1930s. It cannot be discounted that Lenin too would have resorted to at least some degree of force in introducing collective farming; but Lenin would have been unlikely to have collectivised the peasantry at the expense of the lives of the millions who were either 'de-kulakised' or else reduced to starvation in the early 1930s. And yet Bolshevism itself had a predisposition in favour of political, economic and social ultra-authoritarianism; and, even if not Stalin but Trotsky or Bukharin or even Kamenev had assumed the supreme party leadership after Lenin's death, an ultra-authoritarian system of rule would have prevailed. Trotsky, Bukharin and Kamenev—like Lenin—advocated a milder variant of Bolshevism than Stalin's. But it was still Bolshevism.

Admittedly the Bolsheviks were a party whose members in 1917, among themselves, acted relatively democratically—but their orientation in public policy had never been democratic. Indeed their aim was to establish a dictatorship of the working class and the poorest peasants. It requires naïveté of a specially impervious order to deny that this orientation would corrupt the internal life of both the Bolshevik Party and the new Soviet state. All dictatorship corrupts; but totalist dictatorship, even if it falls short of its planned realisation, corrupts totally.

Thus the degeneration of the October revolution is not attributable exclusively to factors outside the control of the Bolshevik Party leadership. To be sure, the intervention of the Allies in the post-October civil war exacerbated political conflict. And the Reds were not the only perpetrators of terror: the brutality of the Whites was equally ghastly. Furthermore, not all the consequences of the October revolution were foreseen or even forseeable by the Bolsheviks (although the Mensheviks had given them warning about several). Even so, these were not the factors which, above all others, brought about the violent and authoritarian 'excesses' which took place in the former Russian Empire in the Lenin era. There really was something violent and authoritarian both about Bolshevism from its inception after the turn of the century and about the October revolution from its earliest days.

A grievous responsibility must be laid at the door of a handful of leaders such as Lenin, Trotsky and Stalin. They formulated the ideas and consolidated the practices which offered land, peace and workers' control to the mass of the population. They truly believed that a new society was buildable which would benefit all mankind. To them it seemed that the dawn of socialism was about to direct its rays across all Europe. But their utopianism had its overpoweringly dark side; and they also found dictatorship and terror entirely congenial.

Yet these figures were not the whole party. They would not have had such an impact if their assumptions had not been shared by leaders at lower levels of the hierarchy of territorially based committees. The Bolshevik Party in the 1920s, the party of Lenin and Stalin, was guided by ex-undergrounders. Such cadres had endured the persecutions of the Tsarist period. They had emerged as tough and dedicated revolutionaries. They wanted to form not a routinised administration but a dynamic, flexible regime which emphasised action at the expense of procedures. They were legal nihilists. As opposition and difficulties mounted after the October revolution, their trust in dictatorship and in the supreme virtues of their own party was reinforced. Ruthlessness gave way to extreme ruthlessness. By the end of the civil war even those central and local leaders—such as Lev Kamenev's sympathisers—who had had trepidations about this approach to the construction of socialism accepted it as natural and desirable. Consequently Stalin found no need, even at the height of his power in the 1930s and 1940s, to draw up a new party programme to replace the Leninist programme of 1919. Stalin altered much in Lenin's policies. Yet he left the party programme not merely unmodified but absolutely intact. It was not until 1961, under Nikita Khrushchev, that a new programme was ordered to be written. Stalin's apparent indolence is not hard to explicate: the basic tenets of the 1919 programme were totalitarian in aspiration.

This same party was united in its fundamental anti-peasantism. Its notions were deeply attached to urban developments, to large scale organisations, to the industrial proletariat. It was united, too, in a commitment to the speedy promotion of the working class to state administrative posts. In addition, it was united by a determination to stamp on the throat of all other political parties both socialist and non-socialist. Not only that: there were lamentably few Bolshevik leaders at the centre or in the provinces who were reluctant to crush the autonomy of trade unions and factory committees from 1918 onwards. The deep streams of a pre-1917 ultra-authoritarianism welled up to cover a massive flood plain.

It is amazing that anyone in the late 20th century can still believe that the Bolshevik Party was quintessentially socialist. A party which could thrust its jackboot into the face of the labour movement, as did the Bolsheviks in their first years of government, has so distorted a conception of socialism that it should no longer be described as socialist.

The people to feel sorry for are not only the workers and soldiers who voted for the Bolsheviks in the local soviet elections of 1917 but also the vast bulk of ordinary Bolshevik party members. Most of them had read no Marx, seen nothing of Lenin and rarely went to party meetings. Socialism was a vague and ill defined concept for most rank and file Bolsheviks. But such recruits, before the October revolution, cannot be shown to have wanted their party ruling Russia dictatorially and alone. Most evidence suggests that 'the party masses' (as the leaders called them, with characteristic condescension) shared the sort of aspirations that most Russian workers had in 1917. An all party socialist coalition was a priority for them. They also wanted both peace and an extension of workers' rights in factories and mines. Many of them left the party in disgust in 1918-19 or else joined the faction that in 1920-1 became known as the Workers' Opposition.

But the rank and filers were outmanoeuvred. In 1917 they had had influence over policies without fully predetermining them. Quickly thereafter they lost even this influence. The cadres from the emigration and the tsarist underground tightened their own command in the one party state. These cadres, contrary to the myth sedulously propagated by those such as Trotsky who sought to explain away their own fall from power in the mid-1920s, were not newcomers to prominence in the party. They were the Old Bolsheviks. They were the backbone of the party of Lenin from the revolutionary period.

It was this party that Stalin inherited, after the intra-party political struggles of the 1920s, from Lenin. Of course, Stalin proceeded to introduce features of his own to party affairs. A difference existed between Lenin's party and the faction within it that Stalin eventually led. Stalin wanted to go even further than Lenin in brutalising Russian politics. Stalin wanted to go faster, and he was going to do it at the cost of millions of lives of completely innocent and unsuspecting people. Stalin's personality was also deeply unbalanced by suspiciousness and vengefulness. He not only wanted to get rid of real enemies, he wanted to get rid of potential enemies as well. He accomplished this aim by means of a mass surgical strike involving the deaths of millions. Lenin's wife, Krupskaya, was to confide to a friend in the 1930s that, if Lenin had not died prematurely in 1924, he would have ended up in one of Stalin's prisons.

All this notwithstanding, the regime that would have existed had Lenin lived longer or had been succeeded by Leon Trotsky would still have been extremely grim. It would still have been a regime which had recourse to terror to secure itself in power and to impose its ideology. It would still have been a regime which was a prison for the peoples. It would still have been a regime with an excess of economic nationalisation, to the point of stifling flair, enthusiasm and practicality. It would still have been a regime which found the technological and output gap widening between itself and the major capitalist powers.

The debate as to whether Lenin led to Stalin, taken in narrow terms, is a non-debate. It is akin to one of those mediaeval theological discussions about the number of angels who can stand on a single pin. Few people even in the middle ages were exercised by angel enumeration. Similarly, hardly anyone nowadays is seriously contending that, as night follows day, so Leninism was bound to develop into Stalinism. But the matter does not end there. Debate rightly exists over the degree and type of continuities that existed between Leninism and Stalinism; and only the wilfully blind would fail to see that those continuities are very strong indeed. Similarly the disputes about the alternative paths of evolution for the party after Lenin's death—Bukharinism, Trotskyism or Stalinism—have an importance not to be ignored. But each strategical option was a Bolshevik one. Each involved journeying down a cul-de-sac of history with no prospect of creating a society without exploitation and oppression.

3

In defence of democratic revolutionary socialism

Samuel Farber

I want to restate some of the key theses and arguments put forward in my book *Before Stalinism, The Rise and Fall of Soviet Democracy* (published by Polity in Britain and in paperback by Verso in the USA).[1]

Without questioning that there were major qualitative differences between Stalin's and Lenin's rule in Russia, *Before Stalinism* shows that, by the time Stalin came to power, soviet democracy had already disappeared. Basing myself on the abundant and mostly recent scholarship on the early revolutionary period, I showed how by 1921, and certainly by 1923 when Lenin ceased to function as the leader of revolutionary Russia, soviet democracy no longer existed. I provide extensive documentation to support this claim not only in relation to the soviets in the strict sense of the term, but also in regard to the press, the institutions of workers' management and control and the unions.

Here I would like to concentrate on two topics which have been mystified or ignored by many in the revolutionary socialist tradition: the trade unions and socialist legality. In the case of the trade unions, *Before Stalinism* specifically showed how Lenin's defence of trade union autonomy in 1921 was no more than symbolic. By this time the trade unions had already come, through the mechanism of party fraction discipline, under the effective control of the Communist Party. In any event, the Eleventh Party Congress in March and April of 1922, the last in which Lenin actively participated, left little doubt about the meaninglessness of Lenin's proposed union autonomy. This Congress resolved that the secretaries and chairmen of the central committees of the unions must be party members of long standing and that the chairmen, secretaries and members of the leading regional trade union bodies had to be party members of at least three years standing. Furthermore, the Congress decided that party members could be co-opted rather than elected to union office. Finally, it was agreed that all conflicts and frictions on union questions would be resolved by the party and the Comintern rather than by the unions themselves.[2] Finally, the notion that there is no need for trade union autonomy under socialism had been established by the Bolshevik majority at a number of trade union congresses that took place before 1921. In fact, as early as the first trade union congress which met at the end of 1917, Zinoviev, who attended the congress as a representative of the Bolshevik Party, made this very claim as a matter of theory and principle. At that congress Zinoviev made an argument that has since become all too familiar, 'I ask you, why and from whom do you need independence: from your own government...?' He also explicitly rejected the right to strike, arguing along the same lines that 'the strike would be directed against the workers themselves'.[3]

Before Stalinism discusses issues pertaining to socialist legality, a topic that many revolutionary socialists would rather not talk about. At the theoretical level, the book criticises Lenin's inclusion of lawlessness as an intrinsic feature of the 'dictatorship of the proletariat', a term which of course refers to a whole historical period and not merely to the violent days and months during and immediately after the overthrow of the old order. At a more concrete and specific level, *Before Stalinism* examines such matters as the post civil war Criminal Code of 1922 which attempted to legalise arbitrary government. For instance, this code continued to uphold the notion developed during the civil war (1918-20) that an act could be considered a criminal offence even if it was not expressly forbidden by any existing law. In addition, the 1922 code allowed for no procedure equivalent to the right of habeas corpus which was meant to ensure that an arrested person was charged and brought before a judge, or else released.[4]

Before Stalinism also examines Lenin's endorsement of collective or categorical punishments, ie terror, during *and well after* the end of the civil war. The term collective or categorical punishment refers to the use of punishment against people who are not even suspected of having been actually involved in carrying out, or helping to carry out, any specific acts against the revolutionary government. Instead, what made these people victims of punishment was that they were thought to share with the possible suspects a common political ideology, party or class membership, or even ethnicity. My book also shows some of the many instances where leaders of the revolutionary government resisted or opposed the use of collective punishments, sometimes even provoking Lenin's anger (eg the Petrograd Bolshevik Central Committee on the occasion of Volodarsky's assassination in June of 1918).[5]

While a student at the LSE from 1961 to 1963 I was a member of the Socialist Review tendency (renamed International Socialism while I was still in London). I still remember our strong arguments against the soviet 'workers' bomb' defended by some Young Socialist comrades. At the time we insisted that the 'workers' bomb' was incompatible with revolutionary socialist principles. Along the same lines, I want to argue that while collective or categorical punishments (terror) are perfectly compatible with petty bourgeois dictatorships (eg Robespierre), let alone capitalist imperialism, fascism or Stali: sm, they are by their very indiscriminate nature unacceptable to a workers' state. There is a major and qualitative difference between measures designed to deprive the former ruling classes of their social and economic power (eg confiscation) and the quite different matter of legally penalising people on the basis of group membership and social origins, rather than of particular criminal or political offences committed by specific individuals. The issue here is not one's love or hatred for the former ruling classes, but what all this reveals about the revolutionary government's legal conceptions

103

and the future consequences of this for *all*.

Western Cold War historiography argued that Stalinism was not that different from Leninism and that the authoritarian character of 'Leninism in power' was already built into the original conceptions of Bolshevism as it was developed at the beginning of the 20th century. *Before Stalinism* clearly and unambiguously rejects such an interpretation. Instead my book endorses and articulates the reasons for the October revolution and also emphasises the fundamentally democratic character of that upheaval. In the process, I argue against several of Rosa Luxemburg's criticisms of the Bolsheviks and show, for example, how the suppression of the Constituent Assembly was quite defensible on democratic grounds.

I also put forward the argument that most of the undemocratic practices of 'Leninism in power' developed in the context of a massively devastating civil war and in fact cannot possibly be understood outside such a context. But while the devastation caused by the civil war is a very *necessary* part of the explanation for the decline and disappearance of soviet democracy, it is by no means *sufficient*. For one thing, the civil war devastation does not explain why the mainstream Bolshevik leadership as a whole made a virtue out of necessity and theorised the undemocratic and dictatorial measures as permanent features of the dictatorship of the proletariat in Russia. This in turn had helped, by the early 1920s, to kill the free and authentic political life of the country, thus depriving soviet society of a variety of possible political defences against the subsequently rising Stalinist monster.

These often programmatic mainstream Bolshevik politics did not just happen 'occasionally' or were simply a matter of 'rhetorical power' as John Rees claims. If Trotsky's *Terrorism and Communism* or Krupskaya's 1923 defence of the crudest forms of book censorship are not in the words of John Rees 'considered analyses of events', what are they then? Lest the reader conclude that these may have been theoretical and political excesses of Trotsky and Krupskaya but not of Lenin, then what are we to make of Lenin's insistence in 1918 that until a German revolution was forthcoming, the soviets should 'study the state capitalism of the Germans,...[and] spare *no effort* in copying it and not shrink from *dictatorial* methods to hasten the copying of it'.[6]

104

Similarly for Lenin's highly undemocratic views (as a rule not justified as temporary measures applying only to the existing situation) as expressed in a wide variety of situations: for example, his reply to the old Bolshevik worker Myasnikov when the latter argued vigorously for freedom of the press in 1921,[7] or Lenin's several pronouncements defending the one party state made during and after the civil war,[8] or Lenin's intervention in the debate over one man management of industry at the time of the Ninth Congress of the Communist Party in 1920. On that particular occasion Lenin in fact argued that whether there was collegial management or individual management on the shop floor was irrelevant to the question of:

> how a class governs and what class domination actually is, [since] the victorious proletariat has abolished property, has completely annulled it—and therein lies its domination as a class. The prime thing is the question of property. As soon as the question of property was settled practically, the domination of the class was assured.

Furthermore, Lenin claimed that there was 'absolutely *no* contradiction in principle between Soviet (that is, socialist) democracy and the existence of dictatorial power by individuals.' (Lenin's emphasis).[9]

John Rees also suggests that the economics of War Communism (1918-20) was merely a desperate reaction to the terrible economic situation facing the Bolshevik government. *Beyond Stalinism* makes it quite clear that the mainstream Bolshevik leadership did not plan for or anticipate the development of War Communism. However, my book does show that once this policy was adopted, initially as a response to the enormous economic crisis facing the country, the government then made a virtue out of necessity just as it had done with the suppression of democracy in the political realm. This was clearly reflected in the mainstream Bolshevik writings of the period and most notably in Bukharin's idealisation of War Communism in his *The Economics of the Transition Period*, a study claiming to be nothing less than 'the process of the transformation of capitalist society into communist society'.[10] As it developed, War Communism did come to mean a dogmatic and absolutist attempt to suppress money and the market and revert to a 'natural' economy of barter and state administrative commands. This new economic philosophy became so encompassing and widespread that it even affected activities quite unrelated to the feeding and physical survival of the population or to the conduct of the civil war. Thus for example in Petrograd, people in need of legal services were not allowed to have any say over their own attorneys and had to accept the one chosen for them by the state.[11]

It is particularly important to underline that War Communism also signified the end of workers' management, control and trade union autonomy. This, however, was no obstacle to the mainstream Bolshevik leadership coming to see the widespread bureaucratic nationalisations of War Communism as a great advance towards the communist goal. It is especially noteworthy that while in 1921 the implementation of the New Economic Policy (NEP) of concessions to capitalism was defined by Lenin as a 'retreat', the disappearance of soviet democracy and workers' control was never so regretted by the mainstream Bolshevik leadership. This does not lead me to conclude that Lenin's mainstream leadership had developed a worked out and hardened political philosophy opposed to workers' management, control and trade union autonomy (as was later the case with Stalinism). I do conclude that in the eyes of Lenin and his co-thinkers these were not defining characteristics of socialism and had a decidedly lower priority than the centralised state control that clearly obtained the upper hand during the years of War Communism. In any case, the political pronouncements of the mainstream Bolshevik leadership in the period subsequent to the civil war cannot be reconciled with what one would have expected from a leadership that did see soviet democracy and workers' power at the point of production as being of the essence of socialism. Among other things, a leadership thus committed to socialist democracy would have repeatedly stressed the temporary nature of the repressive and undemocratic measures and would have spelled out the specific conditions and possible time frames for their removal.

However, my critique of what I have termed 'mainstream' Bolshevism is by no means applicable to the whole of Bolshevism. If anything, my whole book could be seen as a brief in support of Victor Serge's often quoted observation that Bolshevism contained a mass of other germs other than the germ of Stalinism. As mainstream Bolshevism developed new politics in the context of civil war conditions, this was opposed by both the early left oppositionists, (workers' opposition, democratic centralists) and right oppositionists (Riazanov, Lozovsky) inside the Communist Party. As a matter of fact, practically all my specific criticisms of 'Leninism in power' were made *at the time* by one or another revolutionary and most notably by the early Left and Right Bolshevik oppositions. Therefore, John Rees and the Socialist Workers Party leadership's quarrel is as much with the critique of those Bolshevik opposition groups as it is with my own.

> Marx's statement about the democratic nature of the socialist movement...and Lenin's, that revolutionary social democracy represents 'the Jacobins indissolubly connected with the *organisation* of the proletariat' are definitely contradictory. A conscious, organised minority at the head of an unorganised mass of the people suits the bourgeois revolution, which is, after all, a revolution in the interests of the minority. But the separation of conscious minority from unconscious majority, the separation of mental and manual labour, the existence of manager and foreman on the one hand and a mass of obedient labourers on the other, may be grafted on to 'socialism' only by killing the very essence of socialism, which is the collective control of the workers over their destiny.[12]

The fact that the mainstream Bolshevik leadership made a virtue out of the anti-democratic necessities imposed by the enormous hardships of the civil war did not develop in an ideological and political vacuum. Instead, this constituted the exacerbation of a Jacobin *aspect* of Bolshevik politics that became dominant under the stimulus of the civil war crisis.

I would contend that pre-civil war Leninism had two sides that were at odds with each other. On one side was the clearly democratic Lenin who always insisted on the close connection between the struggle for democracy and the struggle for and democratic content of socialism. In fact I believe that Lenin had a better understanding than any of his revolutionary socialist contemporaries of the importance of political democracy as a political goal to be pursued by the workers' movement on behalf of society as a whole. This in contrast to other revolutionary socialists (sometimes including Rosa Luxemburg) who for reasons of economism, workerism or a schematic economic determinism derided the political struggle for general democratic demands such as the right of nations to self determination.

Yet, alongside this emphasis on the struggle for democracy, 107

Lenin and his co-thinkers also held a number of essentially Jacobin ideas particularly in regards to *revolution*. Or, speaking more precisely, a quasi-Jacobin view since Lenin, unlike petty bourgeois Jacobinism, was committed to rooting the revolutionary movement in the politically organised working class. The Jacobin element in this quasi-Jacobinism refers to a heavy emphasis on the will and dedication of the activist minority as contrasted with the weight of *institutions* that encompass that minority as well as much broader sectors of the working class and population as a whole. It is also useful to recall in this context Lenin's repeated tendency, noted in *Before Stalinism*, to solve grave political problems through the appointment of what he considered to be good reliable individuals to positions of power (eg in the Cheka) rather than through the carrying out of structural institutional changes. Similarly, Lenin often tended to see, as in the case of the governmental reforms he proposed towards the end of his rule, the democratisation of socio-economic life solely in terms of promoting leaders and office holders with working class and peasant backgrounds without placing equal emphasis on democratic mechanisms that would make these newly promoted leaders institutionally responsible to popular constituencies. The key problem with Lenin's quasi-Jacobin approach was that the working class, unlike the bourgeoisie, can exercise power in society only *democratically* and *collectively* through institutions such as soviets and factory committees. Thus classical Jacobinism could develop dictatorial power without fundamentally affecting the social or economic power that the bourgeoisie held as *individuals*. However, the moment the working class is deprived of democratic control over the institutions through which it exercises power in society, that working class has lost its power, period.

The Jacobin conception of revolutionary leadership is also incompatible with working class power. To the extent that there exists a Jacobin belief that the truth of the revolutionary activists' vision is sufficient guarantee of their authority to act, to that extent the actions of revolutionary leaders cannot be corrected or reversed by representative popular institutions such as the soviets. This Jacobinism becomes even more dangerously anti-democratic when combined with Hegelian sounding notions such as Trotsky's allusion to the 'revolutionary birthright of the party'[13] in 1921 or the very similar and no less pernicious idea that 'History', in its inevitably progressive development, has reserved *the* role of revolutionary leadership to a particular party or political formation.

While political parties are necessary since they provide indispensable leadership and formulate alternative choices and programmes, it is the representative institutions rather than the parties that must in the last analysis be the repositories of working class and popular sovereignty. From this it follows that the representative institutions must have the ability to *replace* the party in power. While recognising that this would have been, from a practical point of view, a quite difficult task in the conditions of Russia in the early 1920s, I want to stress that the quasi-Jacobin side of Lenin's politics, which became dominant after 1918 and especially after 1921, weighed heavily against his even considering such a possibility *in principle*.

The Jacobin tradition, besides having a strong and uncritical tendency to favour centralisation for its own sake, is not inclined to support the defence of minority rights and civil liberties. While *Before Stalinism* argues that there are of course situations (eg in a civil war) where civil liberties may have to be restricted on a temporary basis, it insists that there can be no real socialist democracy, or for that matter full and genuine innovation and progress, with dissident individuals and minorities terrorised into silence and conformity, and forcefully prevented from attempting to become the new majorities. Today any democratic revolutionary socialism worthy of its name must at the very least cease to regard the defence of civil liberties and the rights of political minorities, both before and after the revolution, as being merely a liberal, let alone 'petty bourgeois', concern.

I began to work on the project that became *Before Stalinism* in 1984, one year before Gorbachev came to power and, of course, before the breakdown of Stalinism and the Soviet Union. I had no inkling that the work I was embarking on would acquire a special relevance within just a few years.

My interest in going back to the 1917-24 period in Russia was a response to political phenomena that had surfaced in the 1970s and early 1980s. On one hand the development of Eurocommunism in Western Europe and on the other hand the rise of a rather distinctive East European and especially Polish dissident political thought which became very prominent after the rise of Solidarity in 1980. These two quite different political traditions coincided in claiming that not only Stalinism but revolution itself was antithetical to democracy. The East Europeans in particular, including people with roots in revolutionary Marxism such as Adam Michnik and Jacek Kuron, borrowed from Karl Popper's idea that the attempt to reshape society as a whole, especially if there is violent action involved, was itself totalitarian. Consequently, democracy was only compatible with peaceful and piecemeal reform. It was hardly surprising that the Russian Revolution was the paradigmatic example chosen by East European dissidents attempting to prove the validity of Popper's dictum. The Eurocommunists for their part also came to the conclusion that they would have to drop Russian 'Leninism' (by which they meant revolution) in order to prove themselves true democrats.

I wanted to demonstrate the compatibility of revolution and democracy. In trying to answer Eurocommunists and East Europeans and taking a closer look at the origins and development of the Russian Revolution I re-examined an explanation for the degeneration of the revolution I had never found fully convincing. I am referring to the views of the left Shachtmanite 'bureaucratic collectivist' tradition and to the British Socialist Workers Party tradition as developed in the 1970s and 1980s. These two traditions, while correctly emphasising the heavy weight of objective factors such as the impact of the civil war and economic collapse, had greatly underestimated the political and ideological sides. The purposes, specific political choices and changes in the political orientation of the main political actors involved had for all intents and purposes been ignored.

I also discovered that these two traditions had unwittingly created a Lenin who was only in part the real historical Lenin. Thus, for example, I found that the very points emphasised by Hal Draper—socialism from below and the importance of political democracy and civil liberties—were a lot closer to the early Right and Left Bolshevik oppositions than to mainstream Leninism. Similarly, I discovered other things that I had never been taught by either tradition: for example, that in 1923, the last year of his life, Lenin had significantly moved in the direction of 'socialism in one country' without of course reaching the extreme of adopting Stalin's later political line.

The collapse of Stalinism, the Soviet Union and most of the worldwide Communist movement has helped to create a radically new situation for the international left. We now find ourselves in a political situation with features similar to the collapse of the

Second International in the years subsequent to 1914. As a result, we are confronted with the task of reorganising the left, a task that we should try to help carry out on the basis of building a new democratic and revolutionary socialism.

I hope that *Before Stalinism* offers the elements of a usable past and will make its small contribution to the rethinking of past revolutionary experiences, a necessary task in this process of reorganisation. In particular we cannot ignore the scepticism and pessimism that the failure of Stalinism has created everywhere. The right wing slogan, 'No more experiments', has had a powerful appeal in the post-Stalinist Eastern Europe. We cannot respond to such a political climate with evasions and Karl Marx's warnings against utopian blueprints—quite justified in the political climate of his day, but today conveying the message that we simply don't have answers to the tough questions that legitimately trouble people.

We know now that a socialist revolution can be lost in more than one manner or fashion. Not only can the revolution be lost to the counter-revolutionary restorationists wanting to re-establish the old order, it can also be lost to a perhaps less obvious but no less devastating counter-revolution—namely, those supporting a new order devoid of democratic control from below unavoidably opening the road for the formation of a new type of ruling class. This can come about because in following the maxim, 'Hold on to power no matter what', power may indeed be retained, but in order to maintain a type of society radically different from the one the revolutionaries had originally fought for.

A socialist revolution in an advanced industrial country may encounter many of the same objective difficulties faced by revolutionary Russia. We cannot assume that a revolutionary takeover will not be preceded by massive destruction, and we certainly cannot expect the ruling classes in industrialised capitalist societies to hand over a carefully preserved intact economy to the revolutionary opposition. Given this and the ever present possibility of civil war, Lenin's challenge to Gorky to present alternative criteria for determining which blows delivered by a revolutionary government were necessary and which blows were superfluous is as relevant today as it was then.[14] I hope *Before Stalinism* can help us to think of how to meet Lenin's challenge.

I would like to conclude this essay by recalling the spirit of the *Socialist Review/International Socialism* tendency with which I am glad to have been associated in the early 1960s. This was a serious, militant and hard working group that with its humility and lack of dogmatism differed dramatically from practically all the other revolutionary groups that I have known in the subsequent 30 years. Least of all did this group suffer from the political obsession of 'hardness', ie the tough macho 'Bolshevik' posturing counterposed to the equally obsessive political 'softness' of social democracy. The SR/IS tendency was also animated by a fresh and creative political spirit that expressed itself in its willingness to engage in a vigorous revolutionary revisionism, eg Tony Cliff on Lenin's theory of the labour aristocracy and on Trotsky's theory of permanent revolution, and Michael Kidron on imperialism. This is the sort of political openness, freshness and flexibility that is necessary in the present period—a period of great crisis for the left but also of great opportunities for those who have new and constructive directions to propose.

At that time Tony Cliff also had a lot to say about the Russian Revolution and its degeneration, and what he said was not contained within the boundaries of Trotskyist or Leninist orthodoxy. I am thinking in particular about the article 'Trotsky on Substitutionism' (*International Socialism*, 2, Autumn 1960), or the book *Rosa Luxemburg* (published as a double issue of *International Socialism* in 1959). The readers of this journal can and will judge for themselves, but I have the strong feeling that what Cliff wrote then is closer to my *Before Stalinism* than to John Rees's 'In Defence of October'.

1 David Finkel has shown in 'Defending "October" or Sectarian Dogmatism?' (*International Socialism* 55) the various ways in which John Rees's 'In Defence of October' seriously mischaracterised the contents of *Before Stalinism*.

2 I Deutscher, *Soviet Trade Unions. Their Place in Soviet Labour Policy* (London and New York, 1950), p65, and Jay B Sorenson, *The Life and Death of Soviet Trade Unionism 1917-1918* (New York, 1969), pp170-71.

3 I Deutscher, op cit, p21, and SA Smith, *Red Petrograd. Revolution in the Factories 1917-1918* (Cambridge, England), p218.

4 I Lapenna, 'Lenin, Law and Legality', in L Schapiro and P Reddaway (eds), *Lenin, The Man, the Theorist, the Leader, a Reappraisal* (New York, 1967), p261, and J Hazard, *Settling Disputes in Soviet Society. The Formative Years of Legal Institutions* (New York, 1960), p314.

5 V I Lenin, letter to Zinoviev, Lashevich and other members of Central Committee, 26 June 1918, in *Collected Works*, Vol 35, February 1912-December 1922 (Moscow, 1966), p336 (Lenin's emphasis).

6 V I Lenin, ' "Left Wing" Childishness and the Petty-Bourgeois Mentality', *Collected Works*, Vol 27 (Moscow, 1965), p340.

7 V I Lenin, 'A Letter to G Myasnikov', 5 August 1921, in *Collected Works*,
   Vol 32, December 1920-August 1921, pp504-9.
8 See, for example, the citations in E H Carr, *The Bolshevik Revolution*, Vol 1
   1917-1923 (London, Pelican Books), p236.
9 C Sirianni, *Workers' Control and Socialist Democracy. The Soviet
   Experience* (London, Verso Editions and New Left Books, 1982), p216,
   and S A Smith, op cit, p228 (Lenin's emphasis).
10 Cited in S F Cohen, *Bukharin and the Bolshevik Revolution. A Political
   Biography. 1888-1938* (Oxford, 1980), p87.
11 E Huskey, *Russian Lawyers and the Soviet State. The Origins and
   Development of the Soviet Bar, 1917-1939* (Princeton, 1986), pp59-61.
12 T Cliff, *Rosa Luxemburg* (London, 1986), p49.
13 I Deutscher, op cit, p55.
14 M Gorky, *Days with Lenin* (New York, 1932), pp44-5.

4

A reply to John Rees

Robin Blackburn

J ohn Rees's article 'In Defence of October' advances a justification of the leaders of the Russian Revolution of 1917-21 and
claims to rebut recent socialist writings which try to draw up
a critical balance sheet of Bolshevism. The contingent justification
of the Bolsheviks is rather well done—but the same cannot be said
of the riposte to Farber, Hobsbawm, Slovo and myself. This having
been said, I must confess I felt absolutely no discomfort reading the
article at all. Rees could have made clearer the evident differences
between those he is criticising, but I did not feel unhappy, either at
being included in their number, or at the occasional selective references to my article. I quickly gathered that the author had a single
minded determination to defend the Bolshevik record and that the
references to myself and others were a sort of polemical garnish.
Writing a piece like this is a considerable undertaking and maybe
the author's adversarial zeal helped him to carry it out. Facile critics of Bolshevism should be abashed by the material it contains
but not most of the left writers that Rees targeted. Perhaps an
author's primary duty is to his own argument, not to doing justice
to everybody else's—though it is always impressive when both
tasks are combined.

I think some comments are in order just in case readers imagine
that Rees really did deal with the arguments of Farber, Hobsbawm
or myself. The interest of these criticisms of Bolshevism surely

arises from the fact that they come from people who, by background and conviction, are scarcely sworn enemies of October. Indeed it may be that most of us still see more in the Russian Revolution to defend than does Rees himself. I would certainly be disposed to credit the Russian Revolution, and the state it established, with playing a critical role in the eventual military defeat of Nazism, with a generally positive contribution to anti-colonial and anti-imperialist struggles, and with providing somewhat more favourable conditions for the Western workers' struggles for better rights and conditions. I am referring here to the broad objective impact of the revolution, and the state it established, not to the particular policies of Soviet rulers who often sought to accommodate themselves to capitalist forces. Strangely enough, John Rees, in his lengthy article, does not deal with such matters which surely have some bearing on the ultimate historical significance of the Russian Revolution.

Rees's defence of October seems to imply two different arguments. Firstly, there is the line of defence which treats the Russian Revolution as a somewhat more sustained Paris Commune, a heroic defeat displaying at once the creativity of popular or proletarian revolution and the barbarism of reaction. On such a view the 'force of circumstance' and stark historical conditions put into the shade the mistake of the revolutionary leaders. I do not think that Slovo, Hobsbawm or Farber would deny that there was an historical grandeur to the Russian Revolution and that Lenin had a far firmer grasp of its political dynamic than the majority of his political opponents.

But Rees seems to be straining for another conclusion, namely that revolutions of essentially the Russian type still offer us a model. For a variety of reasons this is a conclusion that I would strongly contest. The Russian Revolution took place in a society where bourgeois institutions of all types were weak and bourgeois representative democracy a very frail import. I think Rees's own account of the lack of popular esteem for the Constituent Assembly may have a relevance he has not noticed. There are today few countries where bourgeois democratic assemblies are as little esteemed as was the case in Russia in 1917-18. The existence of the soviets meant that the Constituent Assembly did not have the sort of monopoly on general political representation which is the norm for such representative bodies today. Indeed the experience of 'dual power' must now seem to be rather exceptional in the light of the history of the 20th century. In

Russian conditions the backdrop of a crumbling feudal Absolutist order combined with an exceptionally weak bourgeoisie allowed a new anti-bourgeois power to consolidate itself and to bypass the Constituent Assembly, though even in Russia the Bolsheviks themselves paid some tribute to the legitimacy of the Assembly by calling for it to be elected and convened. And they soon discovered the enduring significance of bourgeois representative assemblies in much of the rest of Europe.

Lenin in *Left Wing Communism* and Trotsky in his writings on Germany both memorably warned of the dangers of underestimating bourgeois democracy or failing to establish a vigorous revolutionary presence within it. No doubt Lenin and Trotsky were still inclined at this time to go on regarding the Russian Revolution as a model. But we now have the perspective of a further half century. Fascism was overthrown in Germany and Italy in the 1940s, and in Spain and Portugal in the 1970s, without workers' councils bidding to become rival state structures. Colonialism has been thrown back nearly everywhere without workers' councils playing the key role. Stalinism has been overthrown in Eastern Europe and the Soviet Union without the appearance of institutions of dual power. Hungary had workers' councils in 1956 and Poland had Solidarity in 1980. But if representative assemblies had been conceded would they have been rejected by the Hungarian or Polish working class? I doubt it. France in 1968 and Portugal in 1974-5 did not throw up workers' councils either—in both cases the revolutionary movement was outflanked by the holding of elections to a bourgeois democratic assembly. Saudi Arabia is the only political entity which today might be compared with Tsarist Russia. Perhaps we will see workers' councils there—I certainly hope so—but without depreciating the Saudi revolution I do not think that the rest of the world will follow the same pattern. Where consent of the governed has been solicited by democratic representative bodies I do not think it is either practical or desirable for socialists to imagine that they can be ignored or bypassed. Typically such institutions will be hedged around with a host of undemocratic features and these should be campaigned against by socialists. And situations may arise in which one set of democratic institutions are arrayed against another, weaker and less democratic set, in which case a different sort of dual power will appear. Thus a Scottish Assembly might find itself at loggerheads with Westminster and British socialists might decide to support it. But that would be a quite different scenario to 117

1917. I would imagine that this is what Hobsbawm was driving at when he refers to the Russian Revolution as a 'freak result'.

None of the authors directly criticised by Rees, so far as I am aware, makes very much of the dispersal of the Constituent Assembly. Samuel Farber, who offers by far the most detailed account, stresses that he believes this particular Bolshevik decision to have been justified. What he criticises is the many ways in which the Bolsheviks violated the democratic workings of the soviets—overturning of elections, non-convening of meetings, intimidation of minority currents and so forth. I think his account is a sobering one, raising many serious questions, even if, as I said in my article, I think he does not give sufficient weight to the terrible constraints of the times—both the conduct of the Whites, the ravages of famine and the bloody example given by the supposedly advanced countries in their own Great War. But while I agree that Farber does not take due account of the force of circumstances I think his book is very valuable because it makes it clear what a flawed model this really is and because it draws attention to the existence of currents *within Bolshevism* which contested this or that unfortunate or deplorable decision.

While Farber gives insufficient weight to the 'force of circumstance' argument, he does arouse the lively suspicion that many arbitrary measures were adopted as harsh necessities when they were not actually necessities at all; and, once adopted, there was a tendency to glorify them, so that they became, officially, not harsh necessities at all but expressions of revolutionary virtue and a party minded spirit. In this category could come the celebration of the absence of law as a positive feature of the workers' state, the introduction of one man management in most branches of industry, the wholesale forced requisition of foodstuffs from the peasantry, the falsification of elections to the soviets, the failure to convene the Central Executive of the Soviets, the harassment of even those anarchists and Mensheviks who favoured active collaboration with the Reds, the application of the death penalty, contrary to soviet legislation, to suspects arrested outside the war zone and much else all copiously documented by Farber. Of course by the standards of Ypres and the Somme, or of European colonial warfare, the Bolsheviks could be regarded as quite restrained and humanitarian. But that does not mean that all their arbitrary measures were indeed harsh necessities since, as Farber shows, they were often counter-productive even in terms of beating the Whites and corresponded instead to a sort of Jacobin frenzy, as Rosa Luxemburg noted.

John Rees is shocked at my contention that Lenin was 'not a systematic thinker'. This quote was extracted from a sentence which paid tribute to an aspect of Lenin's thought: 'Lenin, though not a systematic thinker, actually developed a greater grasp than Marx of the necessary complexity of both politics and economics.' What I had in mind here was that Lenin's writings on the party, on the limits of trade union consciousness or on parliamentarism addressed questions which Marx never really considered. On the other hand Lenin did not reconcile what he had said about the party in his earlier writings with what he wrote about soviets in *State and Revolution*. The practice of a party dictatorship corresponded, perhaps, to a certain silence in these texts. While Lenin practised pluralism within the workers' movement he did not theorise it. It was possible to conclude from his writings that ideally there should only be one party, that representing the true interests of workers, in the workers' state. Does John Rees himself subscribe to this view? Indeed I would be interested to know whether the editors of *International Socialism* think that there is a necessary role for law in a socialist democracy. Do they think that workers should have more votes than members of the middle classes, or the retired, or housewives? It may be that I am wrong in supposing that we will not see workers' committees challenge the sovereignty of parliament. I think those who believe this owe us some sort of account of the political principles which would inform these new institutions of a workers' democracy. For my own part I am sure that bourgeois democracy can be greatly improved upon—but not by regressing to assemblies without party competition, or without legal defence of the right to disagree, or without universal and equal adult suffrage. The reader of Rees's critique might suppose that my argument had been comprehensively dealt with.[1] Actually the principal theme of my piece—the need for a workable picture of a socialist economy—was not even mentioned. The Bolsheviks were forced into 'War Communism' by what they saw as military necessity. In the 1919 party programme they committed themselves to intoxicating visions of the suppression of commodity relations. Among other things I try to show that Trotsky came to reject the view that the outright suppression of market relations was either necessary or desirable. His November 1932 essay on 'The Dangers Facing the Soviet Economy' published in the

Bulletin of the Opposition contained a remarkable analysis showing that the power of the ruling bureaucracy was itself based on a voluntaristic attempt to suppress market relations. This might achieve limited goals but would breed great economic irrationality and would be contrary to the interests of the direct producers. While I can well imagine that the editors of *International Socialism* will not agree with the conclusions I advance in this essay I do think they should explain their own view of the sort of economic institutions that would characterise a genuinely socialist economic system. I suppose they would support a system embodying public ownership, planning and workers' control. But would they subscribe to the vision of workers' self management developed by Ernest Mandel in *New Left Review*, 159, or Diane Elson in *New Left Review*, 171, or Pat Devine in his book, *Democracy and Economic Planning*? It is all very well saying that workers' committees are to run everything, but how are prices to be arrived at? What happens when one committee disagrees with another? What assurance is there that 'socially necessary labour' really is socially necessary? Presumably means will have to be found for making producers' views on this question harmonious with the views of consumers (communities as well as individuals). And since socialism can only really exist on a global basis, to what extent would a worldwide planning authority actually control production? How would it tackle the appalling problems of poverty, inequality and ecological danger bequeathed by capitalism, yet not attempt the impossible and undesirable task of prescribing how much of everything is produced, and for whom?

These are the sort of questions which it is now even more necessary than before for socialists to answer, or at least debate. However much we may admire the heroism and creativity of Russian workers in 1917 the revolution itself was eventually lost—and the revolution itself usurped. Those of us who advocate the suppression of capitalism will be expected to explain why we expect things to turn out quite differently next time. And that cannot be done by dwelling only on the heroic aspects of October, and neglecting to consider the ways in which Bolshevism may itself have provided openings for the rise of Stalinism.

1 My essay is reprinted in Robin Blackburn (ed), *After the Fall: the Failure of Communism and the Future of Socialism* (Verso, 1991). While Rees finds me too critical of Lenin, Neal Ascherson, reviewing this book for the *London Review of Books*, 6 March 1992, chides me with being too indulgent towards Lenin and the Bolsheviks. This divergent criticism leads me to believe that I've got it about right. Incidentally I do try to make clear in this somewhat expanded version of my essay that Luxemburg was not wholly in the right in her criticism of the Bolsheviks, though I believe her vindication of pluralism remains fundamental.

5

Dedicated followers of fashion

John Rees

The history of great revolutions is always refracted through the prism of contemporary politics. The English Revolution has long had its hostile narrators on the right and, on the left, its fate has been fought over by Whig and Marxist historians. The relative popularity of these interpretations has been largely shaped by the contours of the domestic class struggle. But the influence of conflicting interpretations of the Russian Revolution has been decided by international considerations: on the one hand the success of popular movements from below, and on the other hand the rivalry between the various imperial powers. Understanding this context is as vital to understanding the revolution as a grasp of the relevant historical facts.

'In Defence of October' was written, not for the quasi-psychological motives attributed to me by Robin Blackburn, but because there is a marked shift in this debate for the first time since the 1960s. The Cold War produced its own viciously anti-socialist orthodoxy and a corresponding attitude to the October revolution—Lenin led to Stalin. The Stalinists had their own reasons for endorsing this view. In the 1960s and 1970s this orthodoxy was challenged, not just by Trotskyists and other anti-Stalinist socialists, but by a number of academics influenced both by social upheaval in the West and by the moves towards detente between the superpowers.

The East European revolutions and the subsequent collapse of the USSR have inevitably reshaped the intellectual landscape once more. The Stalinist model has been demolished—but the right wing, in the historiography of the revolution as in reality, have so far been the major beneficiaries. One reason for this is that many on the left shared some or all of the assumptions about the nature of Russian society which underpinned the Stalinist model and therefore found themselves ideologically disarmed in the face of a newly confident right wing.

Robert Service simply denies that very many 'scholars or commentators nowadays contend that there was an inevitability about the passage…from Lenin to the Stalinist programme of the 1930s'. Two points need to be made about this assertion: i) 'In Defence of October' produced a significant amount of evidence, notably from Stephen Cohen and Edward Acton, to the contrary[1] and ii) Robert Service's own article is testimony that this argument is alive and well.

'Did Lenin Lead to Stalin?' shrinks from using the word 'inevitable', settling instead for the claim that 'only the wilfully blind would fail to see that those continuities are very strong indeed.' The construction of the Stalinist regime is, in Robert Service's account, a single, continuous and unbroken process. The one party state was:

> in a condition of partial construction before the October revolution. The scaffolding for its walls was in place by the middle of the civil war. The roof was added at the inception of the New Economic Policy…

Rarely has the 'malignant straight line' theory (Stephen Cohen's phrase quoted in my original article),[2] received such a concise formulation. Lenin's Bolshevism 'contained many genes which were to produce Stalinism'. Thus, 'even if not Stalin but Trotsky or Bukharin or even Kamenev had assumed the supreme party leadership after Lenin's death, an ultra-authoritarian system of rule would have prevailed.'

But perhaps this is because the desperate straits in which the revolution found itself would have imposed similar policies on anyone who led it? Nothing so historical. The real problem, according to Robert Service, is that 'there really was something violent and authoritarian both about Bolshevism from its inception after the turn of the century and about the October revolution...' So Trotsky merely argued for a 'milder variant of Bolshevism than Stalin's. But it was still Bolshevism.' This is the theory of original sin: Lenin ate of the apple in 1903 and damnation followed in 1917.

Mere historical facts are of little use in combating this kind of reasoning: the judgment has already been made. Nevertheless, it is worth correcting some of the inaccuracies with which 'Did Lenin lead to Stalin?' tries to bolster its metaphysics. Lenin, we are told, did not try to 'terminate' Stalin's political career because he did not recommend his expulsion from the party. Yet surely the removal of Stalin as general secretary was designed to remove him from all effective power. Lenin had rarely recommended anything more severe. Zinoviev and Kamenev, whom Lenin described as scabs and strike breakers for their role in publicly opposing the October revolution, were two of the few prominent Bolsheviks who would have suffered expulsion from the party if Lenin had had his way. But Lenin did not get his way. Indeed, far from being 'bossy' and 'obsessive', Lenin continued to work with Zinoviev and Kamenev, as he continued to work with Bukharin during and after Bukharin led the opposition to the Brest-Litovsk treaty which almost resulted in a split in the Bolsheviks.

Lenin's tolerance for such debate, right up to and including the Tenth party congress, belies the tale that he shared Stalin's desire for a 'single unchallengeable ideology'. Similarly, the contention that both Lenin and Stalin deployed 'terror whenever the party's power was thought to be threatened' obscures much more than it reveals. Lenin did advocate the use of force, predominantly against those who used force, or gave succour to those who used force, against the revolution.

Robert Service's own example of the treatment of Russian Orthodox bishops in 1922 is a case in point. This seemingly despotic act was actually committed in the midst of famine in which a total of 5 million died; the bishops were hoarding gold that could have paid to help feed the starving. The law was carefully framed so that removal of valuables would only take place in the presence of believers and so that no object would be removed that was necessary for worship. Here is a rather less distorted account of events following the proclamation of a law sequestrating church valuables for the aid of famine victims:

> Patriarch Tikhon...branded this law as sacrilegious and non-canonical, and called upon the faithful to resist its realisation with every available means. The agitation which began was carried on in much the same way as the previous agitation against the 1918 decree separating church and state, but with the difference that the issue was now of an entirely humanitarian nature...
>
> To argue the question on the basis of church canons and state laws in a country just emerging from a state of war and revolution and struggling for the very life of starving millions was a futile task. Even legally, religious groups could not refuse to return to the state that which they had received for use only and for which they had signed contracts to that effect...
>
> The conflict that developed between the church and the government, because of the Patriarch's resistance, claimed not a few victims. There were riots with some bloodshed, followed by repressive measures on the part of the state... In all were reported 45 executions and 250 long term imprisonments. The church throughout the country was in a state of anarchy. Large sections of it, particularly in the famine area, resented the Patriarch's stand...[3]

Indeed, when the house arrest of the Patriarch became known, Bishop Antonine and priests Vedensky, Belkoff and Krasnitsky led a group to the Patriarch's residence:

> The day before the execution of the Moscow priests, they appeared before the Patriarch and remonstrated with him that he was chiefly responsible for the terror and the anarchy in the church and that with his name was associated the whole counter-revolutionary policy of the church in recent years. They forced the retirement of the Patriarch and appealed to the church to make peace with the new social order.[4]

But Robert Service is right about one thing concerning Lenin's attitude to the clergy at this time: 'his plan derived not from some definite anti-regime plot.' No, it was the far more important consideration of saving at least some of the millions who were losing their lives. In the end, 'the amount of surplus wealth taken from the church was enormous, and yet so much remains that its loss is hardly noticeable to the visitor'.[5] Naturally one expects that a Professor of History at the School of Slavonic and East European Studies would at least mention this historical context.

Stalin's terror, on the contrary, was not used to alleviate famine. Nor did it defend the revolution or Lenin's Bolshevik Party—it destroyed both. Stalin's terror tried to eliminate great swathes of the population and succeeded in eliminating virtually the entire leadership and many of the rank and file of Lenin's Bolsheviks. Such an internal civil war was necessary precisely because the transition from Lenin's regime to Stalin's state was not simply a quantitative change, as Robert Service contends, but a difference in kind, the difference between a workers' revolution, albeit degenerated, and the emergence of a new ruling class.

Sam Farber objects to being associated with the kind of establishment historical opinion which Robert Service's article represents. He argues that *Before Stalinism* was misrepresented and should have been interpreted as a useful addition to the revolutionary argument. In this, he is echoed elsewhere by David Finkel.[6]

Sam Farber does raise some issues of importance. The first concerns the trade unions. He balks at using the kind of language that Robert Service employs (the party 'thrust its jackboot into the face of the labour movement'), but his argument bears a strong family likeness. The Bolsheviks were anti-union from as early as 1917, claims Sam Farber, quoting Zinoviev's argument that trade unions are unnecessary in a workers' state and noting his 'explicit rejection of the right to strike'.

Typically he does not quote Lenin's 1921 rebuttal of this same argument when it was advanced by Trotsky:

> Trotsky seems to say that in a workers' state it is not the business of the trade unions to stand up for the material and spiritual interest of the working class. That is a mistake. Comrade Trotsky speaks of a 'workers' state'. May I say that this is an abstraction...it is...a patent error to say: 'Since this is a workers' state without any bourgeoisie, against whom then is the working class to be protected, and for what purposes?' Ours is a workers' state *with a bureaucratic twist to it.*
>
> We now have a state under which it is the business of the massively organised proletariat to protect itself, while we must use the workers' organisation to protect the workers from their state, and get them to protect our state.[7]

But perhaps Sam Farber doesn't quote Lenin because he believes this statement to be 'no more than symbolic'? So whose ideas were reflected in the practice of the trade unions, Zinoviev's or Lenin's? Sam seems to have forgotten the answer he himself gave in *Before Stalinism*. There he noted that though there was disillusionment with the unions in the mid-1920s:

> Yet, strikes had not been outlawed. Thus, and even though the unions pursued a no-strike policy, there were reports of 102 strikes involving 43,000 workers in 1921-22, and 267 strikes involving 42,000 workers…in 1924. In 1925 no strikes were sanctioned by the unions but there were still 186 strikes involving 43,000 workers. In 1926 there were 327 strikes involving 32,900 strikers in state industries…[8]

None of this is to deny the very real degeneration of the revolution that was taking place during this period or that such degeneration affected the trade unions. Nevertheless, even when there were formal restrictions on union democracy it would be wrong to conclude that democratic debate on trade union issues did not take place in the key institutions of the revolution. Arthur Ransome, for instance, records the 1920 debate on trade union issues at a conference at Jaroslavl held in preparation for the All-Russian Communist conference. The old Menshevik Larin opposes one man management in industry. After a heated debate:

> Larin and Radek severally summed up and made final attacks on each other's positions, after which Radek's resolution approving the theses of the Central Committee was passed almost unanimously. Larin's four amendments received one, three, seven and one vote apiece. This result was received with cheering throughout the theatre, and showed the importance of such conferences in smoothing the way of the dictatorship, since it had been obvious when the discussion began that a very much larger proportion of the delegates than finally voted for his resolution had been in sympathy with Larin in his opposition to the Central Committee.[9]

After the vote delegates were elected to the All-Russian conference. Larin declined to stand but:

> Rostopchin put it to the conference that although they disagreed with Larin, yet it would be as well that he should have the opportunity of stating his views at the All-Russian conference, so that

the discussion should be as many-sided as possible. The conference expressed its agreement with this. Larin withdrew his
withdrawal, and was presently elected.[10]

Of course discussions like this are not the same as discussions
inside the trade unions themselves and Sam Farber is quite right
to point to the spread of the practice of appointing union and
party officials by the mid-1920s. But he is hardly original in
making this point. Indeed the 'mainstream Bolshevik tradition',
which he is so keen to denigrate, made precisely these points.
Trotsky's first attack on the bureaucracy, partly in response to a
wave of strikes in Sormovo, Kharkov and the Donets Basin,
insisted that:

> The present regime...is much farther from workers' democracy
> than the regime of the fiercest period of War Communism. The
> bureaucratisation of the party apparatus has developed to unheard
> of proportions by means of the method of secretarial selec-
> tion...dissatisfaction...does not dissipate itself by way of influence
> of the mass upon the party organisation (election of party com-
> mittees, secretaries, etc) but accumulates in secret and thus leads
> to interior strains...[11]

Socialist legality is the second issue which Sam Farber raises.
Again he will not quite use Robert Service's phraseology (legal
nihilists), merely insisting that Lenin saw 'lawlessness as an
intrinsic feature of the "dictatorship of the proletariat".'

So were Lenin and the Bolsheviks monsters with no care for
the justice or otherwise of individual cases, simply arresting and
executing people because of their class origin? 'In Defence of
October' showed that Lenin completely rejected this idea when
it was advanced by Latsis, one of the leaders of the Cheka, and
cited a series of incidents where Lenin personally intervened to
correct injustices.[12] To this we can add instances recorded in John
Keep's recent and largely hostile account of the early months of
Bolshevik rule.[13] The first incident involved the murder of two
leading Cadets by anarchist sailors. Keep tells us Lenin took
this seriously, 'bombarding the investigators with requests for
information (nine actions from 7 to 31 January)'—but that in
the end the case fizzled out since the perpetrators could not be
found.[14] In a second incident Lenin backed strenuous investiga-
tion into accusations of arbitrary searches and profiteering by Red

Guards, although he was by no means convinced of their guilt.[15]

But what of the wider question, raised both by Sam Farber and Robin Blackburn: do revolutionaries stand for the systematic and equal application of the law? It would be easy to give the glib answer—that any democrat, let alone socialist, wants to see justice done and that this involves people knowing what the law is and only being prosecuted for demonstrably breaking it. That is certainly what we would wish to be the case in a socialist society. But such a situation can only exist where there is a social consensus to the effect that the law makers and the system of justice are legitimate. In capitalist society most of the time the ruling order, through a mixture of force, fraud and propaganda, can convince a large enough section of the population of their legitimacy to enable the 'rule of law' to prevail. A revolution and civil war are, by definition, times when no such consensus, and therefore no such legitimacy, exists.

The case of the bishops who hoarded church riches, cited above, is an example. Despite their explicit recognition of the separation of church and state, despite signing legal documents that the church riches now belonged to state agreed trustees and despite the Patriarch's public guarantee not to enter the political arena, the church took the first available opportunity to break all such undertakings. And it did not break them in a way which would allow simple police methods of arrest and trial to deal with the question. It chose methods of class warfare—calling on its followers to use any available means to resist the government.

Faced with such situations, and the revolution and civil war were replete with far more dangerous examples than this, the Bolsheviks moved between trying to establish a socialist legal framework and themselves having to use the methods of open warfare. And in warfare individual justice (did this particular soldier point his rifle at me and am I therefore justified in shooting at him in reply?) is inevitably replaced by categorical judgments (is he or she on our side or not?).[16] One wishes for the former, but cannot rule out the latter. It is for precisely this reason that I recorded the judgement of such a hostile witness as George Leggett in my original analysis:

> in the inevitable clash between the arbitrary violence of the Cheka and the system of Soviet law evolved by the People's Commissariat for Justice, the Cheka gained the upper hand whenever the regime

came under threat; when crises receded the [People's Commissariat] won the advantage.[17]

Sam Farber objects to having his account of the revolution likened to those of the right wing. In one sense of course he is right: Sam's *intention* is to strengthen the socialist tradition, not to bury it. But he nevertheless uses arguments which are close relatives of those deployed by the right because he rejects 'mainstream Bolshevism' and because his analytical method is badly flawed.

Sam's rejection of 'mainstream Bolshevism' is conducted under the banner of a possible alternative outcome of events which he sees latent in the criticisms of Lenin advanced by the Right and Left Bolsheviks in the 1920s. The chapter in *Before Stalinism* entitled 'Alternatives to Lenin' has sections dealing with Right Bolsheviks, Left Bolsheviks, anarchists and Left Social Revolutionaries—but no section on the Left Opposition and only a handful of references to Trotsky. So when Sam claims that 'all my specific criticisms of "Leninism in power" were made *at the time* by…the early Left and Right Bolshevik oppositions' he is right. But he has chosen to construct a retrospective ahistorical alternative composed of a pick and mix of all their programmes. Now, of course, if there were an animal which was half sheep and half pig we could happily carve pork chops and lamb chops from the same carcass. The Left and Right Bolsheviks had mutually incompatible programmes in every area—foreign policy, the peasantry, the economy, military affairs—which is why an effective opposition could not emerge until Trotsky built an opposition based on an economic and social, as well as democratic, alternative to the bureaucracy.

But *Before Stalinism*'s search for an alternative to mainstream Bolshevism is not really to do with the history of 1920s Russia. It is to do with political organisation in the 1990s. Sam Farber rejects Lenin's model of the party as 'Jacobin'—and since this conception of the party was with Lenin since at least 1902, and since Sam Farber clearly believes it was an important cause of the degeneration of the revolution, it is pointless, though understandable, for him to deny that his thesis bolsters the right wing's claim that 'the authoritarian character of "Leninism in power" was already built into the original conceptions of Bolshevism'.

131

The charge of Jacobinism is itself misguided. The authoritarian nature of the societies established by bourgeois revolutions does not, in any case, stem primarily from the political forms of organisation adopted by the revolutionaries. Rather both are a function of the fact that the bourgeoisie is itself a minority, albeit leading a majority against the old order, and therefore tends to develop such organisations as can mobilise the masses but at the same time represent the bourgeoisie's own sectional interest against the masses.

The need for a revolutionary party springs from the quite different profile of the workers' revolution. Here the problem is that although the revolution represents 'a movement of the immense majority, in the interests of the immense majority', the process by which a class moves into struggle and becomes politically conscious is both uneven and lengthy. If the minority of revolutionaries created by day to day struggles are to survive and to have influence on the subsequent course of the struggle they must necessarily organise themselves, even though they are for the time being a minority. How this minority becomes the majority involves the whole body of revolutionary strategy and tactics. Clearly there are dangers, both that the minority will become impatient and substitute itself for the class and that it will become demoralised and dissolve itself or blunt its revolutionary politics. But this problem cannot be wished away with talk of Jacobinism.

Such political positions carry a methodological dimension. Sam has accomplished the astounding feat of writing an entire book about the rise of Stalinism without ever saying exactly what sort of society he believes Russia had become by the 1930s. Was it a new class society, state capitalist or what? The answer to this question matters because if you see the rise of Stalinism involving a social counter-revolution then the economic and international isolation of the regime became crucial because it deprived the Bolsheviks of the material basis for socialism. If, however, this is not the case it opens the way to locate the transition to socialism only, or mainly, at the political level. This seems to be Sam Farber's position as his quotation of Rakovsky's point about income differentials and political influence being the defining characteristic of the bureaucracy indicates.[18] Further evidence for this interpretation comes from the way in which *Before Stalinism* locates the origin of such repressive societies as China, Cuba and Vietnam. These 'revolutionary leaderships', we are told, 'made conscious political choices favouring undemocratic political arrangements...not as lesser evils imposed by...economic and other objective difficulties'.[19]

All this, in turn, opens the way for an analysis of the October revolution which insists that democracy, legality and a socialist constitution could have turned the tide where Trotsky failed. Hence Sam's summary of his position:

> the moment the working class is deprived of democratic control over the institutions through which it exercises power in society, that working class has lost its power, period.

There is no gainsaying this as a general statement, but it utterly fails as an account of the degeneration of the Russian Revolution. In this context it would be far more accurate to say that *the moment the working class ceases to exist as a social force even the most democratic institutions will lose their power over society.* The isolation of the revolution meant the destruction of the working class in the civil war and the famine that followed—which is why concentration on the purely political is not an antidote to determinism but a failure to observe the most elementary requirements of the Marxist method.

Since Robin Blackburn relies exclusively on Sam Farber for his interpretation of the October revolution, I hope that I have already supplied adequate replies to at least some of the issues raised in 'A Reply to John Rees'. He does however go on to raise a number of questions about the contemporary relevance of the October revolution which require a response.

Let me begin by giving answers to two direct questions posed by Robin Blackburn: does the tradition in which *International Socialism* stands believe in socialist legality and a plurality of parties and do we have any analysis of the kind of economic structure which a socialist society would entail? The first point is easily answered. Of course we believe in socialist legality and a plurality of parties—and so did the Bolsheviks until the darkest days of the civil war. But, as I have already said in my reply to Sam Farber, to win such freedoms requires victory in a class struggle. Only on that basis can the consensus necessary for the operation of any form of legality be established. And in that struggle the laws of battle will sometimes contradict the rules of polite debate. Our chances of success are greater than those faced by the Bolsheviks for the very good reason that we hope to be at the head of a working class that is the overwhelming majority of the population, not one which numbered merely 3 million out of a total population of 160 million, and in an advanced industrialised country, not in a still largely peasant land.

The economic structure of a socialist society cannot be fully examined here. But Robin Blackburn is mistaken in believing that it has not been a subject of discussion in our tradition. The Bolsheviks' early attempts at a mixture of state guided and market mechanisms were referred to in 'In Defence of October'. Robin Blackburn himself has noted Trotsky's writings on the same subject. Related issues have been examined by Chris Harman in 'The Myth of the Market' (*International Socialism* 42), and Alex Callinicos who devoted a considerable part of his book, *The Revenge of History*, to the kind of political and economic structure that a socialist society might need.

But Robin Blackburn's major objection to 'In Defence of October' is that it argues that the Bolshevik experience still supplies us with a model for a socialist strategy today. This is mistaken, the argument runs, because the Bolsheviks failed to appreciate 'the enduring significance of bourgeois representative assemblies in much of the rest of Europe' and could only pursue a successful revolutionary strategy in Russia because 'bourgeois institutions of all types were weak and bourgeois representative democracy a very frail import'. Of the great revolutionary upheavals of the 20th century only Hungary in 1956 and Poland in 1980 have given rise to genuine institutions of workers' power and even these could have been dispersed easily enough if a bourgeois democratic set up had been granted.

One immediate result of Robin Blackburn's analysis is that the collapse of the distinctive features of class politics, whether of the reformist variety or of the revolutionary tradition, is taken to extremes. 'In Defence of October' noted that one result of the left wing attacks on the Bolshevik tradition was that 'much of what now passes for socialist thought is indistinguishable from run of the mill liberalism'. Sadly, Robin Blackburn has all too quickly provided a striking example.[20]

The historical 'facts' which supposedly underpin this shift are quite wrong. In the all important German Revolution of 1919-23 workers' councils were ranged against bourgeois parliaments. The decisive factor in the defeat of the revolution was the inexperience of the revolutionaries, not the legitimacy of the National Assembly.

The Finnish revolution of 1918 failed for similar reasons, as did the Spanish revolution of 1936. In Chile in the early 1970s the inter-factory committees, the cordones, threatened to become an alternative centre of power for the working class to that of Allende's left wing government, and this in a country known as 'the Britain of Latin America' for its supposed stability. Similarly, whether the crises in France in 1968 and Portugal in the mid-1970s developed into revolutionary situations was not, in the final analysis, a question of loyalty to bourgeois institutions but of political leadership, although not simply in a narrow or immediate sense. A decisive factor in many of these cases was the influence of Stalinist popular front politics—strangely, the very politics Robin Blackburn is so keen to see revived in the form of Charter 88.

It should scarcely need saying that the legitimacy of bourgeois democracy even in the advanced capitalist states rests not on some timeless historical loyalty on the part of workers but largely on their ability to sustain the standard of living of the population. Yet this is a time when even American workers have lost 17 percent of their real income in a generation, when the core of the European economy, Germany, is more unstable than it has been at any time in the post-war period, when the great series of recessions which opened in the early 1970s shows every sign of deepening and when the great bogey of the Stalinist states has vanished. As I write, Los Angeles is under a curfew enforced by tanks and over 10,000 troops, a fact reported in *The Observer* under the headline 'Superpower Retakes Gutted Second City' and with the words, 'The upsurge of anger in New York and a score of other cities showed how precarious the normal order is'.[21] It seems a poor time to be arguing, Fukuyama style, the historical inviolability of bourgeois democracy.

What connects all these responses is that they are written by people who have altered their appraisal of the October revolution under the twin impact of the fall of Stalinism and the collapse of the enthusiasm which was generated by the struggles of the late 1960s and early 1970s.[22] Then fashion dictated at least a sympathetic hearing for the Bolsheviks if not outright identification with revolutionary politics. Now intellectual fashion—for there have been only essentially minor revelations of new historical facts about the revolution[23]—dictate a different tune. Transitory notoriety can be attained by such methods but the socialist movement requires more constant companions.

1 'In Defence of October', chaptre one of this volume, pp15-16, 24.

2 Ibid, p24.

3 J F Hecker, *Religion and Communism* (London, 1933), pp207-20. I am grateful to Mike Haynes for this reference.

4 Ibid, pp209-10.

5 Ibid, p209.

6 David Finkel's contribution to the original debate was remarkable if only for its tone. Why he should have chosen to write in a particularly abusive form is a mystery. Those interested can find his article in *International Socialism* 55. Perhaps one reason is that he overestimated the degree to which 'In Defence of October' was directed at *Before Stalinism*. Eight references out of a total of 270 hardly constitutes a 'running polemic'. Nevertheless, let me deal with the points he raised:

References 1 and 2: the first objection is that I accuse Sam Farber of believing that Lenin's pre civil war policies led to Stalin, the second that I deleted 'Farber's explicit specification of the period after the civil war as a focus of critical political analysis'. This point is particularly easy to deal with since David Finkel provides the refutation on the next but one page. Finkel reproduces, at slightly greater length but with no alteration in meaning (supposedly his second objection), the passage in which Sam Farber tells us that Lenin's distaste for codified rules 'had sometimes played an important role in his political practice concerning internal party organisation'. Finkel then adds: 'Examples are then cited from old factional battles between 1903 and 1909'. In other words, Lenin's pre-1917, never mind about pre-1921, policies are being used as evidence for his 'chronic distaste' for legal procedures. Finkel comments that 'obviously, this has *nothing* to do with the caricature...that the Bolsheviks were some kind of monolithic party'. Readers will have to judge for themselves how obvious this is.

Reference 3: This is a lengthy quote from 'In Defence of October' which even Finkel admits 'quotes without blatant distortion'. He then goes on to wonder about things that I 'imply', ie things that Finkel wishes I had said but which in fact I did not say.

Reference 4: concerns my supposedly ignoring the fact that Lenin and the Bolsheviks did not call the introduction of War Communism a retreat (as they did the introduction of the NEP). Yet 'In Defence of October' clearly quotes Lenin complaining that the nationalisation policies under War Communism were forced on them and that if they continued 'we shall inevitably be beaten' (p53). I also quote a Bolshevik leader of the Food Commissariat talking of food requisitioning, the other major social policy of War Communism, in these terms: 'What do you think, the People's Commissariat of Food Supply does this for its own satisfaction? No, we do it because there is not enough food' (p55). The forced, makeshift nature of War Communism is clear enough from contemporary statements, even without looking at Trotsky's and other Bolsheviks' later depositions on the accidental nature of developments in this period.

As to the use of the phrase 'Stalinist Leninism', I still maintain that no one keenly aware of the counter-revolutionary nature of Stalinism, of the river of blood running between the revolutionary tradition and the Stalinist tradition, should dream of employing such an expression.

Reference 4a and 4c: David Finkel clearly believes that when I quoted Farber on the White Terror my omission of the words 'in this context' was a 'cynical manipulation'. On the contrary, it does not alter my point at all; it is the omission of a full discussion of the White Terror which is a 'cynical manipulation' of the real history of the Russian Civil War, and to do so in the name of isolating the 'political dimension' is to compound bad history with bad method. The same technique is used in the discussion of the Green Terror. Here the impact is even greater since knowledge of the brutality of the peasant risings is less widely known than that of the Whites. *Reference 4b*: 'In Defence of October' claimed that Sam Farber quoted Latsis but did not quote Lenin. David Finkel's quotation from *Before Stalinism* shows that I was right—Farber mentions Lenin's objection in a phrase of two words and does not quote him. This lessens the impact of Lenin's forceful intervention and is typical of the way in which *Before Stalinism* uses a qualifying phrase to disguise the importance of the key episodes in the development of the Lenin government.

7 Quoted in T Cliff, *Trotsky* Vol 2, *The Sword of the Revolution* (Bookmarks, 1990), pp176-77.

8 S Farber, *Before Stalinism* (London, 1990), p88.

9 A Ransome, *The Crisis in Russia 1920* (London, 1992), pp52-3.

10 Ibid, p53.

11 *Documents of the 1923 Opposition* (London, 1975), pp2-3.

12 'In Defence of October', op cit, p53 and p51.

13 J Keep, 'Lenin's Time Budget: the Smolny Period' in E R Frankel, J Frankel and B Knei-Paz (eds), *Revolution in Russia, reassessments of 1917* (London, 1992).

14 Ibid, p348.

15 Ibid, pp350-51.

16 Warfare is a suitable analogy, although the dangers of mistaking your enemy in a class war are obviously greater than in a conventional military struggle. Farber's analogy with the workers' bomb argument is, however, potty. We can say with a high degree of certainty that an exchange of nuclear weapons would destroy the working class, and that the use of categorical punishment, however undesirable recourse to such action might be, would not.

17 'In Defence of October', op cit, p65. Although Leggett is exaggerating in describing all Cheka operations as arbitrary violence.

18 *Before Stalinism*, op cit, p5.

19 Ibid, p3.

20 Although I did not dream that within a year Robin Blackburn would have carried that process so far as to call on socialists to vote Liberal in those constituencies where Labour was not best placed to beat the Tories in the British general election of 1992—advice which, if followed, would allow the Liberals to erode Labour support in exactly the way that the Labour Party built itself at the expense of the Liberals in the early decades of the century.

21 The *Observer*, 3 May 1992.

22 This is even true of Robert Service, whose best book, *The Bolshevik Party in Revolution* (London, 1979), was contemptuous of 'Robert Daniels, Leonard Shapiro and Merle Fainsod' who 'portray Bolshevik ideology as the original sin and regard Lenin as the greatest sinner' (p6).

23 One of the few exceptions is M Reiman's *The Birth of Stalinism* which, basing itself on German archives, shows that the Trotskyist opposition was stronger than previously thought and just how complete the break between Stalinism and the revolutionary tradition had to be.

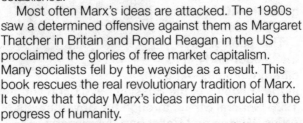